CAT AND MOUSE (SHEEP)

IN PRAISE OF PROGRESS

A LITTLE SATIRE

A MONOLOGUE

Gregory Motton

PLAYS THREE

CAT AND MOUSE (SHEEP)

IN PRAISE OF PROGRESS

A LITTLE SATIRE

A MONOLOGUE

OBERON BOOKS

LONDON

First published in this collection in 1999
by Oberon Books Ltd. (incorporating Absolute Classics)
521 Caledonian Road, London N7 9RH
Tel: 0171 607 3637 / Fax: 0171 607 3629

Cat and Mouse (Sheep) first published by Flood Books in 1995

British Library Cataloguing-in-Publication Data
A catalogue record for this book is available from the British
Library.

ISBN: 9781840020212

Cover design: Andrzej Klimowski

Typography: Richard Doust

CONTENTS

INTRODUCTION, 7

CAT AND MOUSE (SHEEP), 21

IN PRAISE OF PROGRESS, 87

A LITTLE SATIRE, 159

A MONOLOGUE, 197

INTRODUCTION

Men must learn now with pity to dispense
For policy sits above conscience.

(Timon of Athens)

I n these three plays we see Gregory Motton grow into the mature satirist he has always promised to become. Satire is a hard form to bring off in any medium but it is especially so in a play, where it has tended to be driven by a melancholic central character, often the author's persona, at the expense of real drama. Its other trouble is transience, which is why its recent history in particular is largely one of glibness and superficiality. The still-born farragos of Howard Brenton and Tariq Ali bear cruel witness to this. The truth is that real satire must be timeless, or perhaps more to the point it should fragment time.

The satirist's past, present and future must all collide with the drama's external concerns for reasons of interest and vitality. The only targets worth hitting are moving ones and to do that you have to be moving yourself. This means abandoning yourself to your own torrent of bile with its corresponding backwash of tenderness and love. It also means exercising discretion and discrimination, a requirement too often forgotten in the eighties as political satire descended to the level of lazy abuse. As Swift put it in his *Verses On His Own Death*: 'He spared a hump or crooked nose/ Whose owners set not up for beaux.'

Like all satirists Gregory Motton offers resistance to the pieties of the day. But he is painfully aware that you cannot just attack them with another set of received ideas. The true satirist knows that the best way of showing how stinking and corrupt a government has become is by examining what those who conspicuously oppose it are up to. Genuine resistance is always a step away and often consumed with its own crazy dream of power. Motton negotiates these ironies with something like the dialectic of Brecht, only it moves at breakneck speed so that you can hardly see it in his increasingly polyphonic dramas, the first in this book being *Cat and Mouse (Sheep)*.

Cat and Mouse (Sheep) returns to the more public and political concerns of the earlier *Ambulance* and *Downfall*, both reminiscent in their surreal outrage of the 'guerilla' theatre of Imamu Amiri Baraka (Leroi Jones) and perhaps Genet's *The Screens*. But he preserves much of the domestic canvas of *A Message for the Broken Hearted* and *Looking at You (revived) Again*. In fact those two bitter fragments of neurasthenic romance provide an emotional index for all of Motton's plays: the prison of a set of relationships and responses which stay the same changing only their form – the personal and sexual – the crippling received ideas of those outside this poisoned circle – everyone else – and the soul's ability to transcend the above – dreams and the unconscious. What else could he have called it but *Cat and Mouse (Sheep)*? And yet beauty and timelessness must be pursued, however unpromising the actual facts, or you simply oppress the audience with your opinions. Indeed Motton's most vicious satire is reserved for those who persist in believing that the actual facts are different, a growing number as we slide into the infantilism of the late nineties. Motton often strikes close to home, which wins him few friends. Here Gengis the shopkeeper comes in shock to his aunty:

> GENGIS: Aunty I have begun to notice a sublime look upon Uncle's face. Perhaps he has discovered this enlightenment you speak of? And just now, well it must have been an apparition...
>
> AUNTY: Dreamy boy what did you see?
>
> GENGIS: Uncle, in a small room with what appeared to be... friends
>
> AUNTY: One of his workshops
>
> GENGIS: They were waving their arms in the air

AUNTY: Just a warm up dearie to prevent it all
   becoming too headbound

GENGIS: And when I asked what they were doing
   they turned at once and looked at me with strange
   hollow eyes

AUNTY: They were probably just tired Gengis
   darling, your uncle is a terrible bore when he's
   helping people express themselves

GENGIS: But Aunty, there was a strange sense of
   evil in the room

The semi innocent Gengis has witnessed a cultural phenomenon; his opportunist Uncle reinvented as workshop leader instructing his charges in the virtues of not thinking. Indeed the workshop is part of a world where self or group expression is generally considered better than thinking. Of course this approach has a terrible record in this century alone. But Motton's argument is not with therapy, relaxation, massage, drama groups and so on, all of which can be beneficial, but rather with those people who have a vested interest in suppressing intellect and literacy and thinking for yourself: the sheep. Motton surveys a world where stupidity reigns even in places where the whole point is that it shouldn't or at least not exclusively; theatres being a prime example. Self-expression rather than thinking may now be education's aim, but the range of what is being expressed is always the same. An individual imagination has no means of cultivating itself as we drown in the repetitive, ever-changing sameness of our lives, until we no longer speak with our own voices or notice what passes for our thoughts. Being a sort of compound persona weakens our very sense of being alive, emphasising the chemical and fleeting nature of existence, Webster's 'a little crudded milk/Fantastical puffpaste.' Even that group of natural outsiders, Asian shopkeepers, are being sucked in; so much so that Gengis's price war with the shop next door – he's selling chickens and cold drinks cheaper –

is so successful that he takes over the country and becomes its monarch, although his wife Indira walks out with the baby because she 'hates a money grubber, hates me hates herself hates the baby hates the flat hates the single bed hates shops hates life'. Gengis's Uncle and Aunty remain as hangers-on and functionaries of sorts, sniffing a world where you can get rich quick more than once and really fuck people over. The language of totemic culture blasts through Uncle's mouth in a litany of excitement and pain. What is he? Man? Woman? Aristocrat? Asian? It doesn't matter anymore. He knows that what matters is how much like shit you can make other people feel. That's politics today, says Motton. And he's right.

> UNCLE: I hate weak men. So don't come to me,
>   because I look after number one k?ok?ok?ok?ok?
>   So don't blubber just because you want to be
>   mothered because it's not on offer so watch out
>   because this is the cultural revolution and what's up
>   is going to be down and what's down is going to be
>   down even further, but all in name only because do
>   you know what? Betting is immoral and those
>   weaselly little Irishmen in the betting shops should
>   be taken out and put to work digging holes in the
>   road and made to do aikido. I'm doing a class in
>   social awareness, Fuck you, you racist!

As Gengis observes, Uncle is only after a bed of his own here, rather than sharing the single with him and Aunty now that his wife and baby are gone. However, behind Uncle's speech lies the satirist's age-old question: what's wrong with vulnerability and a kind of uncertainty? In the 'fuck you' culture we live in, Uncle knows unconsciously that just about everything is wrong with it. It's no accident that one of the play's main analogues is Hamlet. Gertrude, Claudius, the cloud shaped like a whale, all have their equivalents here where you have, similarly, to invert someone's words to discover the truth. In certain moods Gengis himself provides the moral corrective. When the Arts Council style laureate Dickwits says of his own poetry; 'I think you will find that it makes people sit up straight when they hear it', Gengis counters; 'If I want someone to sit up straight I'll put a railing up their arse.' Supported on this occasion by Uncle and Aunty he goes on to say that in his view art in this country is controlled by 'Miss fucking Prim and Proper'. It's hardly surprising that the ever-growing number of self-styled producers who populate the corridors of our subsidised theatres fear Motton. It's proof, of course, that the satirist is doing his job; but as *Cat and Mouse* demonstrates you are more likely to be praised for what you do badly rather than what you do well. Miss (or Mr) Prim and Proper specialises in driving the sane and decent mad, elevating the mediocre to giddy heights, and calling the arch politician sensitive and kind. Pope knew this, Swift did. They knew something more though; and so does Motton as his beautiful and tender coda to the play shows. Gengis's wife Indira is returning at the head of a large force, as Gengis and Aunty reach the end of the tether.

> GENGIS: What happens when the seed begins to grow?

> AUNTY: The clouds begin to fill with snow

> GENGIS: What happens when the snow begins to fall?

> AUNTY: The birdy sits upon the wall

> GENGIS: What happens when the wall begins to crack?

> AUNTY: The stick falls down upon your back

> GENGIS: What happens when my back begins to bleed?

> AUNTY: Then you are dead and dead indeed

> GENGIS: What happens when the cat's away?

AUNTY: The mice begin to play

AUNTY tiptoes off.

GENGIS: Aunty I'm frightened

GENGIS stands on the chair with the rope around his neck.

Although it is principally satire, *Cat and Mouse (Sheep)* is also a drama of the heart and the unconscious. Motton's post-election play *A Little Satire* shows what's happened to public as well as to family life. Would Gengis's Uncle have applauded a New Labour victory. Or is he a New Tory? 'I'm a justice fanatic, a fan, I wear the right clothes, I'm left-wing, I'm anti-semitic I'm anti this I'm anti that I'm a star fucker and I'm interested in crystal balls and pot-pourri and Che Guevara and Mussolini and Winnie Mandela.....' There was a time not so long ago when people merely took their thinking off the shelf. Now the shelf unloads itself directly into their brains, and there's a new deposit of poison on that shelf daily. We then dispense this poison in a tone of cynical detachment with any emotional content in heavy quotation marks. What about all those workshops to release the feelings? Where do those feelings go? In Motton's play the various political parties offer only different versions of the same disease: guilt, indebtedness, self-loathing. Unless of course you're as blame-free of everything as lovely Tony, and wear an expensive jumper with a teddy bear on it. But in the midst of his rightly vicious play about vile politicians and a stupid, ignorant populace, Motton brings forth a boy who calls for what we all might really like:

> Beautiful architecture and culture and old things and new things and peace and freedom and homes and food and fields and flowers and we give presents to everyone and stay home Sundays and give thanks to the creator and talk to all the happy animals and trees and walk in the paths of wisdom and a quiet spirit and dream of the mists and forests that covered our land and the sunshine and old stones of other

lands where our forefathers were and be happy and
one with all peoples our brothers and sisters and we
remember old dances and old songs can you do that
for us mister?

Motton's play is a lament for the loss of idealism, which in its
true form is what Coleridge meant by 'good sense'. Every last
idealist, it seems, has been purged from view, laughed off the
face of the earth as childish and naive. Perhaps as Bresson
commented about the future of cinema, the revolution can
only be forged by 'a new breed of young solitaries'. The boy
declares to the canvassing politician that he's thirty-six years
old, therefore ironising what he's just been saying. But it
remains just true enough and no satirist can leave the field
open for one voice only. *A Little Satire* cruelly exposes the fact
that the 90s language of caring disguises the truth that there
has never been less love in human beings than now. It is a plea
for love but also and perhaps more importantly for 'good sense'.

The as yet unperformed play *In Praise of Progress* is also a
plea of sorts; perhaps for an end to the unending upset that
flows through the earlier *A Message for the Broken Hearted* and
Looking at You (revived) Again. The new play's love triangles are
broken, fathers withdrawn, dependencies shattered. There seems
only a faint hope the mess can be pierced, and yet the play has
a mildly redemptive air. Motton combines his personal and
public satire in such a way that it reminds you of nothing so
much as an Ayckbourn for disinherited humanists (with a
religious overtone) who've panicked or turned nasty; the
grovellers in the shadows of the world New Labour cares about,
the human marginalia who don't qualify as politicians or
opinion-formers like Gerry Adams or Liam Gallagher. In short
the play is partly about people with unfashionable lives and
unfashionable thoughts but with more style and talent than
New, or even Old Labour's chosen few. Yet these non-chattering
stragglers are not spared Motton's satire. As foolishness,
seriousness and failure are outlawed, panic and hysteria are
rising steadily in their ramshackle colonies. People are really

going over the edge. Soon the sin of being less than comfortable on this earth will mean forfeiting one's right to healthcare and public transport. Despite appearing to rebel Motton's characters have absorbed and participate in a world where neurosis has finally replaced sensibility, chivalry, even honour, as the only means by which human beings can conduct their daily struggle, with themselves and each other. All personal concerns now have to be retracted through an idea of popular culture that renders them external, and therefore hopelessly alienating. No occasion, however small or large, can smack of itself; its essence must be externalised and purged. We judge ourselves by the standards of a hysterical conformity in a manner that is truly neurotic. Motton spreads his nervous response to his condition – our condition – among pained personae who miraculously appear as fully-rounded characters. It's also remarkable how such pitiless terrain can sound rich echoes of *The Tempest,* Shakespeare's most bitter and healing play. Motton's downbeat Prospero, the less than flourishing Mr Greenhouse, presides over a household that has seen better days. He has two children, positive Marvin and lambent Bubbles; their mother has fled to Barcelona. A former lover of Mr Greenhouse, the heartbroken and violent Mrs Fischbein, comes to a party at the house. Mr Smith seeks the hand of Bubbles in marriage. Bubbles and Mr Smith met on the banks of river where each was watching a boy being hanged and drowned by a mob, an incident which Mr Greenhouse is keen to hear about at his first meeting with Mr Smith. He begins, however, with a little fatherly badinage belonging to a vanished age but his emotions are strangely at odds with the gesture.

> You're very welcome here Mr Smith, my daughter has told us all about you – not happy she says. That's alright with me, neither am I. In my younger days I used to be happy, I once laughed for six months non-stop

We are back in the poisoned, but on occasion charmed circle familiar from *A Message for the Broken Hearted*; oblique sexual violence threatening any possibility of family life. Greenhouse sits at the centre of the circle with the non-combatant's frown, exposing the shame and fragility of his family, and dourly puncturing the aspirations of those who orbit it for one reason or another: Mr Smith, Mrs Fischbein and several others. Mr Greenhouse both revels in and despises the sadness of his own family romance. Bubbles is a little infected with the finality of her father's preoccupations, probably at too young an age. But her stillness and steadiness – a resoluteness that many find irritating – can expose the sham in others. She can see how Mr Smith's habitual irony, especially in the field of compassion, has shrunk his world. His apparent lack of feeling has become just that; a lack of feeling. The force of her intermittent concentration on his emotions makes him confess, perhaps because he thinks she wants to protect him, provide sanctuary from his broken psyche.

> MR SMITH: My eyesight is twisted with suspicion
>
> BUBBLES: You've lost your compassion you mean
>
> MR SMITH: Exactly. I thought I had it but it was gone. I kept it hidden to preserve it but it went rancid, it rotted away. I forgot where to find it and in the end I could only find it by the smell
>
> BUBBLES: Alright, that's enough
>
> MR SMITH: The stench, the terrible stink of cruelty. The crueller I am the more compassion was once there and has been lost
>
> BUBBLES: I understand already
>
> MR SMITH: And then, even the cruelty faded away and I became lazy and ignorant, a fountain of bile
>
> BUBBLES: Stop now
>
> MR SMITH: There are scenes between people no-one should ever see

BUBBLES: Then just don't tell anyone

MR SMITH: And one more thing. What if I lost
you and couldn't find you?

BUBBLES: Then you would go to my house and
find me there. You have no need to worry

Bubbles knows that evasiveness is a trap. Mr Smith knows it
too. But he also knows that a feeling at birth is already an
opinion about yourself, the other person, the music scene. It's
hardly surprising that Mrs Fischbein has reached the pass she
has. 'I don't want to be tolerated I want to be adored. I want
someone who will never let me out of their sight, who will
follow me accross the room with their eyes. And that is a way
of being free Mr Smith. You're not listening to me at all.....'
Motton anatomises these modern dilemmas with humour as
well as ruthlessness. The seventeenth-century playwright John
Ford knew that where feeling is concerned the breakdown of
the medieval religious and symbolic order would ensure that
we live forever in a conflict between warring individual
definitions of emotion and love that threaten to breach
"th' unguarded castle of the mind". If two people can't agree
about what an emotion is how can there be a relationship?
Each private ritual, however tiny, is now more or less an
attempt at universal domination. Where Ford employed
Burton's *Anatomy of Melancholy* as an index to the disintegrating
self, Motton writes in the eye of a capitalism so advanced that
it has blown up even the last vestiges of the bourgeois self,
which has been just strong enough to survive up until now. In
this context Mr Smith is still fighting the world, while the
vaguely Jungian Mr Greenhouse with his vision of cow birth
and his Barbara Hepworth style sketches opts for a sort of
quietism in his own living room. He tries to explain this to
the dangerous ex-lover, the once fish-slaughtering painter Mrs
Fischbein, whom he describes as 'miraculous' when he first
met her. She accuses him of living for maudlin thoughts, to
which he responds:

MR GREENHOUSE: I live for joy, yes joy. The
    joy of life

MRS FISCHBEIN: The joy of life?

MR GREENHOUSE: That's right

MRS FISCHBEIN: And where is it?

MR GREENHOUSE: It's here. In my house

This is one line of resistance, however passive, but as the party
goes out of control with a little neighbour girl murdering three
people in the house and Mrs Fischbein enticing the hook of
Mr Smith, the play's sheer pressure and velocity works up a
whirlwind that jettisons it into surreal and fantastical realms.
But it never really leaves the living room or exists outside the
minds of its central protagonists. And yet an outsider, Mr
Smith's employer Mr Baron, a kindly soul, expresses the reverse
side of satire in a speech even more moving than the boy's in
A Little Satire:

MR BARON: Yes but what I say is, what is wrong
    with a long list? Let it be long in the name of
    Christ, let it be long enough to include all that
    is there, before it all disappears. And if you
    don't want to name something then don't,
    leave it out, but don't say it doesn't exist. If
    I jump into this river now and say that I am a
    fish, then let me swim like a fish, feed me with
    fish food, sing fish songs to me and catch me
    on your hooks, but don't say 'fish have gills
    Mr Baron, not lungs'; Fry me if you like, pour
    remoulade on my back, but don't say I didn't
    love water! Because I DIED when you took
    me out of the water so I do love water!

The play has a lyric code in which the image of a fish is
central. But the first three plays in this volume have a code.

Each line, each image, connects us back to the whole. This is not to say that the plays are about their titles or an implied metaphor, or at least no more so than Ibsen's *Ghosts* or *Look Back in Anger*, but rather that each part of them corresponds to an overall image as in a painting; and Motton is a very painterly writer. His characters speak in numerous voices and inhabit a thousand attitudes; but in the emotional frieze of the whole they have extraordinary clarity; but it is a clarity that eludes definition. In fact his plays make us anxious to define things less, except perhaps if we do so by means of Mr Baron's infinite list. But that would require patience, humility, discretion and love; all of which we find on the other side of the satirist's coin.

A Monologue, the last play in this volume, is a natural coda to the three full-length plays. The speaker, who has been brought to a room to await the millennium, inclines to irony, but struggles for a directness in his dawn thoughts, which could be titled 'meditations in a time of emergency', after a dead poet. The dusty figure, consuming a breakfast laid on by his millennial hosts, disarms us by saying:

> Amongst my generation there was no more willing a participant than myself. As a child I remember thinking: "They're going to really like me!"

The memory of the child's elation at the possibilities of life collides with the speaker's astonishment at discovering that, in his part of the world at least, adult life is governed by a sort of false euphoria, which makes a mockery of childhood's unabashed elations:

> Childhood was an unfortunate invention. Now everyone wants some of it, it's spread. Now we have to walk and talk and think exactly like children.

> You wouldn't have thought it possible but there it is.

> The Venerable Bede wouldn't have thought it possible but there it is.

The discoveries of childhood have been externalised. They no longer exist in each new startled imagination. You can wear them like a new suit of skin whatever age you are. The speaker of this monologue believes that celebrating the millennium is like this: sweep away the dust, see no evil, pretend that life is an exciting story of technological development. Look at all the cheap plastic rubbish we buy our children with such an insane sense of purpose. The speaker is frankly worried by the massive collective blindness he sees all around him. Though he appears to be doing nothing but eating his breakfast and noting various noises, including a solitary bird singing, his warning is terrible:

> ... and when there's a cheaper way of disposal it *will* be used, it must be used, in the interests of hygiene and conservation. You are in the pulveriser and your minced meat is about to be fed to the sheep

Motton's antithetical persona waits for the millennium, but sees nothing to celebrate, because nothing is called by its right name anymore. The terror and the joy of life have been concealed. If the Nazis had known the word 'restructuring', they would surely have used it, covering as it does a multitude of grimy sins. The modern credo could be 'say whatever you like as long as it is a lie.' This is the ruse of the living who hide all traces of the dead whom, the speaker observes, have no need of lies. Or rather it is the ruse of those living acquisitively; those with no desire to share the world with the dead or their residue of knowledge, tradition, wisdom, perhaps humility:

> "But these living men" says I, "are so reckless, this life they lead is all destruction. Why between them they have knocked down every thing, ploughed up beauty and torn down grandeur and homeliness alike"

Motton's dusty philosopher dreams he speaks with God, who tells him he did not give humankind an afterlife. On hearing this, he reveals that he himself is an avenging angel of a kind: impelled to correct humanity's defective sight. There is irony in the conceit, but Shelley too saw the poet-philosopher in this light. It's difficult though, for anyone to take themselves seriously in this role as the millennium approaches. Most are happy to fall in with the extraordinary inversion of human values that rules our lives. Even the man who as a child thought "They're really going to like me" can only think of "several who are not in agreement, misfits, failures and the insane – in fact my friends and family!" He had imagined he might have been singing at the gates of Heaven with his friends and associates: singing clear, pure songs of joy and piety. But he isn't; he is forced to celebrate to death:

> "Such a fantastically exciting time! – someone in fact said to me. But I ignored the remark because the person was insane"

A Monologue should be performed as a matter of urgency; but on second thoughts perhaps it shouldn't be, as it has every chance of being thoroughly and wilfully misunderstood. Gregory Motton still awaits his audience.

Simon Usher
London, 1998

CAT AND MOUSE (SHEEP)

Characters

GENGIS

UNCLE

AUNTY

DICKWITS

MAN

OLD WOMAN

CAT AND MOUSE (SHEEP) was first performed at the Théâtre de l'Odéon, Paris, on the 1st April 1995. It was directed by Gregory Motton and Ramin Gray, with the following cast:

GENGIS, Kevin McMonagle

UNCLE, Tony Rohr

AUNTY, Penelope Dimond

DICKWITS, MAN, OLD WOMAN, Patrick Bridgman

Designer: Nigel Prabhavalkar

Lighting: Robert Longthorne

Sound: Laurence Muspratt

A small greengrocers. A seventy-year-old woman comes into the shop.

OLD WOMAN: Three pounds of aubergines please

GENGIS: Ah a dinner party I suppose?

OLD WOMAN: That's right, a few meat-eating friends are coming round so we're having a big chicken salad

GENGIS: Sounds super

OLD WOMAN: Can I have a bottle of cherryade on tick?

GENGIS: Certainly. Are you a bit short?

OLD WOMAN: Yes my boyfriend has been made redundant again. That's the fifth time this year.

GENGIS: Do you want these? They're alright but they've gone a funny colour. I usually make a stew with them

OLD WOMAN: Mmm thanks. How m–

GENGIS: No have them

OLD WOMAN: Oh thanks

She pays for the aubergines and then goes.

GENGIS: I'm going to sell chickens in future

UNCLE: But next-door sells chickens

GENGIS: I can sell them cheaper

UNCLE: He'll be annoyed

GENGIS: He shouldn't charge so much, people round here can't afford it

UNCLE: He's greedy

GENGIS: He had that new floor put in for no reason, now he's got that loan to pay back

UNCLE: He's got to walk on something I suppose

GENGIS: What was he walking on before?

UNCLE: That's a good point

GENGIS: It's all his own fault

UNCLE: So, the gentleman's agreement is going to come to an end is it?

GENGIS: I've got to make a living too

UNCLE: You'll be stocking milk next

GENGIS: I will, and cheaper too

UNCLE: He'll be very put out

GENGIS: I can't help that anymore

UNCLE: It'll be war on this parade

GENGIS: And another thing

UNCLE: What's that nephew?

GENGIS: I'm moving out of that flat of his upstairs

UNCLE: Yes well it could be embarrassing, what with this price war and all

GENGIS: I'm sick of paying the rent

UNCLE: But where will you and Indira and the little horror live?

GENGIS: We'll live in the back room here

UNCLE: But it's only tiny. All of you in one small room. How cramped it will be!

GENGIS: We'll get by

UNCLE: But there's no window

GENGIS: We're rarely in, we're always here working

UNCLE: But there's no running water

GENGIS: There's a tap in the yard

UNCLE: There's no toilet

GENGIS: We'll go in a bucket and I'll carry it out to the nearest convenience

UNCLE: What does Indira say?

GENGIS: She's very excited

UNCLE: Darrin

GENGIS: Yes uncle?

UNCLE: Where will your aunty and I stay?

GENGIS: You can sleep in there with us

UNCLE: What kind of bed is it?

GENGIS: A large single

UNCLE: So that's you, Indira, Aunty, the baby and me all in one single?

GENGIS: A large single. I get up early anyway so you can all stretch out

UNCLE: Hardly stretch

GENGIS: Come and have a look

UNCLE: You've got the bed in already?

GENGIS: Yes, you'll be surprised how roomy it is

UNCLE: Alright

They go and look in the back room.

Pause.

They return.

UNCLE: Yes you're right. It's quite spacious after all

*   *   *

UNCLE: Well, how's it going with the old price war?

GENGIS: Things have changed a lot uncle

UNCLE: I see he's started stocking vegetables

GENGIS: I don't mind that. He still can't do 'em cheaper than me. And the quality of mine is better. I don't sell rubbish you know

UNCLE: He sells those bags of potatoes

GENGIS: They're rubbish they are. I've got all cold drinks in and jars of pickle and all the Indian stuff. It goes like a bomb

UNCLE: You've changed too. You're ambitious, a man building an empire. Do you think you're still the considerate chap you used to be?

GENGIS: I'm giving people good food cheap. I never rip anybody off

UNCLE: But what if he goes out of business? Then they won't have a grocer around here, they'll lose out. You'll never be able to stock everything he does. Everyone will have to walk miles to Sainsbury's

GENGIS: He won't go out of business, not if he watches himself

UNCLE: Life is harder now. I don't sleep

GENGIS: But we've got more money

UNCLE: But I don't enjoy spending it anymore. I feel sorrow. Your aunty, she's always been a swinger, she loves the high life but I'm more your man with a book beside the fire, a bit of an intellectual, studious, high-minded moral type, a rear guard man, a thinker,

a political animal, a fabian, a fundamentalist, I'm a
justice fanatic a fan, I wear the right clothes, I'm left
wing, I'm anti-Semitic I'm anti this I'm anti that I'm
a star fucker and I'm interested in crystal balls and
pot-pourri and Che Guevara and Mussolini and Winnie
Mandela and co-operatives and things you stick on the
fridge and notes and notelets and note pads and living
in London because there's a really thriving bi-sexual
community there and lots going on and I own my own
home and I run a little car because I care and I could
really fuck you up if you get in my way brother sister
mother black white racist sexist bloody bastards the
whole lot of them, call me Ms don't fuck with my
possessions OK because they're all approved and
everything's kosher and I'm on the right side of the
fence and I don't read much but I like a good book
about suffering Chinese or suffering anybody anyplace
because you know what I mean, there's so much
suffering isn't there and I earn a bit of extra cash
working for this charity organization that recycles shit
and sends the best of is to the niggers and magically
makes a massive profit and that's OK because they're
helping people and I believe in that so I'm doing my bit
and earning a fast buck at the same time, that's the future
you know, recycled rags for the little babies with flies
on their eyes. We're all going to be so fucking rich and
so fucking pleased with ourselves my pussy is going to
explode with pure satisfaction and that's all you can do
isn't it because the world is going to rack and ruin. It's
criminal, it's a crime, people have to be free, you know
what I mean, they have to think for themselves, I always
do. All I want is enough money to do exactly what
I want because the state owes me a living course they
do course they do course they fucking do. I pay my
taxes, I'd willingly pay more, I was a bit of a punk
rocker in my day, I went to all the gigs and I stapled
my thumb, anyway they're all arms dealers and so would

I be because deep inside I'm a poetical sort of a person, I'm a lyrical sort of a person, I'm a sensitive sort of a person, I'm a creative sort of a person and I know how to get some if you want some, but I've lost all interest in sex and I'm proud because I'm not going to be exploited and if I had any kids I'd put bromide in their tea because it's all about degradation and men bore me and so I just say "look" you know what I mean and he said "look baby, it's all just words, you're so afraid" and I said "typical man, look at the way you're dominating this argument" and then like the poof he was he went and cut his own throat with a Financial Times letter knife. I hate weak men. So don't come to me, because I look after number one ok?ok?ok?ok?ok? So don't blubber just because you want to be mothered because it's not on offer so watch out because this is the cultural revolution and what's up is going to be down and what's down is going to be down even further, but all in name only because do you know what? Betting is immoral and those weaselly little Irishmen in the betting shops should be taken out and put to work digging holes in the road and made to do aikido. I'm doing a class in social awareness, Fuck you, you racist!

GENGIS: So uncle, what you are saying is you want a bed of your own

UNCLE: Yes

GENGIS: Alright I'll see what I can do

*   *   *

UNCLE: Your silken purse my darling is voluptuous to my fundament

AUNTY: Our nephew. He's like a tub of cream cheese

UNCLE: He's beautiful

AUNTY: Life is beautiful Ned

UNCLE: You're not uncomfortable with the new activities?

AUNTY: He's getting very frenzied in his movements, do you think he's gone mad

UNCLE: He's a man of the people if they did but know it

AUNTY: I hate people, they're so unfair and horrible. Give me animals any day. A little doggie for example, all hair-cut and shampooed doing its little shitty in my hand, aaah the poor love!

UNCLE: Shsh here's Gengis

AUNTY: Gengis darling, you look so low

GENGIS: Indira has left me

AUNTY: Oh no! Did she take the kid as well?

GENGIS: Yes

AUNTY: Thank God. I hate their shitty little bottoms. Are you a broken man now?

GENGIS: She said I'd made a big mistake, that she still loved me, that she'd never come back, that she hates a loser, hates a schmuck, hates a money grubber, hates me hates herself hates the baby hates the flat hates the single bed hates shops hates life

UNCLE: You've upset her haven't you

GENGIS: There's no going back now. I've nothing else to live for. I must put up new shelving

AUNTY: Darling

GENGIS: Yes?

AUNTY: Have you forgotten the charm of a quiet life?

GENGIS: Yes, completely. All I want now is destruction and victory and failure and death and victory and suffering and defeat and death and victory

AUNTY: Are we going to stay open later in the evenings?

GENGIS: We'll never close we'll never open. This will be 100% total shop, neither shop nor no shop

UNCLE: There's greatness in those words, Aunty

AUNTY: There's greatness in the lips that speak them

UNCLE: Greatness in the tongue and eyes that invent the words and send them to the teeth that cut them. The temples of his mind, the soles of his feet. He's ours now Aunty, our own boy

GENGIS: I am king

UNCLE: You are the Royal Emperor

GENGIS: I am khan

AUNTY: You are a cunt

GENGIS: I will die a cunt. I will die, the world will laugh. Blood will gurgle in that breath and the world shall expire with me

*   *   *

In the palace of the mighty Khan.

GENGIS: Uncle take me away from all this. I want to laugh and sing, I want I want to pull the legs off flies and burn them with a magnifying glass like the other children

UNCLE: Here take my hand Barry. I want to tell you something. Look around you son, what do you see?

GENGIS: Not much actually

UNCLE: That's right my boy because do you know? There isn't much left. There used to be things, but as you know it's all been either broken or sold or sent somewhere else. There were things here boy that scum like you wouldn't recognise if it slapped you in the face. You hear what I'm telling you boy, you hear what I'm sayin'?

GENGIS: Yes I do sir

UNCLE: When I was your age this wasn't just paradise on earth this was the peak of fuckin' human achievement. We didn't just have busses, no sir we didn't just have flower fuckin' beds, though you bet your sweet life we had 'em, yes sir we had 'em. No we had something else. Shall I tell you what that something else was nephew child?

GENGIS: Tell it Sir

UNCLE: We had philosophy! Yes! We had art. Yes! We had politics and history and sociology; we had *MUSIC*. I can hear it now callin' to me over th' airwaves. There was music in the streets and parks, there was music in the stores and booteeks, at the railroad stops and the city squares and in the gleaming white hospitals full of ailin' folk a' convalessin' you know what we had there? You guessed it boy – Ding dong, pling plong bing bong dow de dow dow. We had white arsed muthafuckrs singin' the blues and blue nosed nigra fellas singin' their selves purple, we had chinkies that were kinky with their rinky tink tinky and Puerto Ricans and Mohecans makin' sounds that were out of bounds. And if ya didn't like it you know what ya did boy?

GENGIS: No sir

UNCLE: Ya went and ya fucked yourself, yes sir that's what yer did 'cause there wasn't no way no place you could git away from it because The People Were Telling It Like It Was you know what I'm sayin'?

GENGIS: I reckon I do unk

UNCLE: Now listen me boy and listen me good. I ain't gonna continny this here con-ver-sation. I ain't gonna go on an' itemise all of them things we had back there in th' good old golden days cuz I might embarrass you. I ain't

gonna say like as we had them librarees where folks
come and pessued theys lernin and a-readin and a-lookin
up thungs because there ain't no muthafuckr kin read no
more in this nation

GENGIS: Get to the point uncle darling

UNCLE: The point is that what little remains of the great
civilization that once held sway here I want you to think
of as yours to dispose of how you will

GENGIS: I shall do

UNCLE: Good

GENGIS: What's that great blue thing outside the window
uncle?

UNCLE: The sky

GENGIS: Remarkable how it's changed. You see how it
now seems to have a head and out of the top of its head,
why look, it's raining!

UNCLE: Is it? No, that's a whale

GENGIS: Is it true they are why you can't get a council
transfer even on medical grounds? Because they've given
all the flats to the whales?

UNCLE: Yes it is true

GENGIS: What rotten luck for the plankton

UNCLE: Listen carefully boy; The plankton are scum. Evil
and lascivious. They know nothing, feel less. My plan is
to infect the gorgeous belly of the spermy leviathan with
their odious little bodies until they are all beached, the
mucousy little white scum and the great blue monster of
carnal desire together. Then we shall haul them to the
knackers' yard and make them into glue for my model
aeroplanes

GENGIS: But Aunty told me the whales cry most beautifully. Real tears. She has tapes

UNCLE: All fakes. Merely an ingenious amplification of her bowel movements set to music

GENGIS: She's a woman of many pretentions my aunt. Shall I have her liquidated?

UNCLE: Not yet boy, she may want to buy something. Now before I forget I want you to strip to your underwear

GENGIS: But uncle darling I told you I need time, sweet words, the odd bunch of flowers. I want to feel needed first

UNCLE: Gentle boy, be at ease, this is a purely altruistic deed on both our parts. You see, this fax came in

GENGIS: What is it? It's so beautiful!

UNCLE: It's a photo of an earthquake in Turkeytown, 10,000 dead

GENGIS: Hmm, if you hold it upside down they all seem to be languishing most charmingly on piles of jauntily arranged furniture and possessions. Where is Turkeytown, can we go there?

UNCLE: Sorry son it's too far. It's a land without borders in heartiest Afrique

GENGIS: What a golden land. Do you think they'd like to buy something?

UNCLE: It's possible, but we must move swiftly. The quake was followed immediately by a terrible civil war

GENGIS: Heavens! We must help them!

UNCLE: Then a famine

GENGIS: Lord have mercy!

UNCLE: Then a surge of their national debt

GENGIS: Christ have mercy!

UNCLE: And a plunge in their credit profile

GENGIS: Lord have mercy! What shall we do?

UNCLE: Put your clothes in a brown bag and we'll mail
them with a press release

GENGIS: Marvelous idea. I get it; the first one free, the
rest they pay for

UNCLE: That's it

GENGIS: (*Stripping.*) Hmm I feel good. I feel excellent.
Now I'm bored. I'd like to go and exhibit myself

UNCLE: A trip to the theatre. I'll book tickets at once
(*Phone.*) Hello Wally? What's on? – Hmm "loins"
a challenging exposé of a decade's housing policy,
a thought provoking musical

GENGIS: I like it

UNCLE: Or, a radical reworking of the bard's great tragedy
"Omlette – You can't make one without breaking eggs."

GENGIS: I like it better

UNCLE: 25 tickets please, yes. We'll have a row to
ourselves

GENGIS: Goody, we can crawl along the seats to each
other waggling our tongues like this (*Waggles his tongue.*)

UNCLE: Excellent boy!

GENGIS: All I want is my fingers around the greasy pole

UNCLE: And then?

GENGIS: Work it gently to see what I can get out of it like the other members of my parliament

UNCLE: What if nothing is forthcoming?

GENGIS: Then I shall take to the streets in protest

UNCLE: It's almost unprecedented for a head of state to get involved in demonstrations

GENGIS: I shall have the army with me of course

UNCLE: It may just swing opinion your way. There is a lady to see you

GENGIS: I must strip search her at once (*Pulls on rubber gloves and a WPC helmet.*)

AUNTY: Gengis darling!

GENGIS: Aunty it's you

AUNTY: May I have a little word?

GENGIS: Of course, what is it?

AUNTY: Well you see, you know how I love art, you know how I've always had loads of friends who are very clever and one lovely girl called Janet-with-crabs?

GENGIS: Yes, that well-known working girl

AUNTY: Well we've made a little experiment with my doggie's doodoos

GENGIS: Yes

AUNTY: We've made a weally weally big pile of it and made it all dry in the sun

GENGIS: That's lovely aunty

AUNTY: And now it's as big as a house

GENGIS: Wow

AUNTY: And well, Janet-with-crabs and I thought the little people who live in the horrid smelly bit of town would like it in their little smelly park, because they love their doggies too and they also love their doggies' doodoos, I know they do because they spread it everywhere, even outside the food shops, they love their little doggies they do

GENGIS: Yes

AUNTY: And you know how Janet-with-crabs is such a friend of the people and all her work is done to help them because you know she is people too you know she told me and she used to talk like this eeow eeorw eeow (*A strong London drawl*)

GENGIS: Did she?

AUNTY: Yes and now although she talks like us now she's still like that inside, she said so, even though of course she's not really because she likes all the things I like, we're like twins

GENGIS: Yes

AUNTY: Well we took the big big pile of doggie doos and put it in their tiny tiny park and the nasty scum are so thick they said it was a nasty pile of doggie doos and take it away they said, take it away and they said Janet-with-crabs, Janet-with-crabs all the time over and over and I cwied!

GENGIS: Well aunty, they are too stupid. Your pile of doggie doos is wasted on them

AUNTY: That's what I said, I said to Janet-with-crabs let's bring it here to Gengis and put it in his front room or in his garden or in his little lovely pretty park in the lovely northern suburb of H........ where he lives because he is king

GENGIS: No fucking way! What do I want a pile of dog shit here for, I've got enough with that little crap machine you pull around on a lead leaving its disgusting mess everywhere. My Samarkand calf slippers are ruined. Now fuck off

UNCLE: There is a rude man to see you oh great philosopher king

GENGIS: Send him –

UNCLE: O mighty wordsmith of the soul

GENGIS: Send him –

UNCLE: O illustrious moral engineer, jack of all trades

GENGIS: Send him my regards but I have a lunch appointment

UNCLE: He is most importunate

GENGIS: I am sorry for him

UNCLE: He is the very picture of frailty

GENGIS: Give him a –

UNCLE: He's idle, he's poor, he has everything

GENGIS: I'm running a fever, my clothes are sticking to me

UNCLE: He is most spectacularly downtrodden

GENGIS: He is a dreadful bore, send him away

UNCLE: My lord he is green with envy

GENGIS: Is he?

UNCLE: Glowing like an emerald

GENGIS: Poor man send him in

UNCLE: This way dog and make it snappy

MAN: Good afternoon O dainty one

GENGIS: You have made a horrible smear on my lino, you are much to blame. Now quickly, you have a suit for us?

MAN: The people have sent me to say this to you; we are all slaves –

GENGIS: Stop right there. I will have no such ignoble word used inside these walls

MAN: Then we are the vilest... servants... kicked like dogs –

GENGIS: Have some self-respect man, don't affront my ears with such filth

MAN: What shall I say?

GENGIS: Don't say slaves or vile servants. Say you are journeymen. Stand upright, start again

MAN: We are journeymen –

GENGIS: Wait. I think apprentice is better

UNCLE: Start again

MAN: My Lord, the people have sent me to say we are apprentices –

GENGIS: Stop again. I think apprentices has a bad odour. Doesn't it put you in mind of a horrible hierarchy of status. Let him say 'we are master craftsmen'

UNCLE: Say master craftsmen

GENGIS: Sorry, let him say guildsmen

MAN: My Lord we are guildsmen –

GENGIS: Good I am pleased

MAN: – and our children are starving, we are beaten daily and our old folk are thrown into the streets, our cripples are made laughing stocks and our idiots are molested in

all manner of ways by everyone. We languish in
degradation and confusion, we are less than brutes,
less than savages, we are like the quickening flies
on a dung heap

GENGIS: Don't say cripple, say Sedate

MAN: Sedate my liege lord?

GENGIS: Yes, not lissom or agile perhaps, not acrobatic
and frantic in the way of the younger healthier
guildsmen, but still sedate

MAN: I –

GENGIS: For remember; I may be a spastic in my head but
my body glistens from tip to prick

UNCLE: Un bon mot, mon petit!

GENGIS: Do I complain? Do I use ill-sounding words to
slander my brothers? Do I use the words of a pink nose
brown shorted blue shirt red neck dupe? No. I have put
my house in order. I suggest that you do the same,
before you prejudge, predetermine and interfere with
your brothers and sisters. I think you understand me,
we'll none of it

MAN: No My Lord

GENGIS: Now, was there anything else?

MAN: Yes, I wondered if Your Majesty required une fille à
champagne?

GENGIS: A what?

MAN: Une cocotte au compot

GENGIS: Eh?

MAN: A tart My Lord, my daughter

GENGIS: Ah yes, send her in

MAN: At once O Mighty One

Goes.

GENGIS: Nice fella. A bit thick. And, if I'm not mistaken, a spic, a greaseball, a wop and a dago. Stank the place out. Time for the royal bath

*   *   *

GENGIS: Aunty and uncle... Why?

AUNTY: Because we love you

GENGIS: I do want a companion

UNCLE: A girlie?

GENGIS: Yes

UNCLE: What about the prime minister?

GENGIS: Too early a riser to satisfy me

AUNTY: (*Thrilling at his words.*) We're winning, we're winning, we're winning the battle against loneliness. Can you lend me the price of a cuppa?

GENGIS: Wait, where are my ambassadors?

UNCLE: They're on their ways

AUNTY: They have jet lag and are sleeping it off

UNCLE: How shall we amuse ourselves until their return?

GENGIS: Perhaps I can meet the executioner?

UNCLE: He's busy just now. Here, read this

GENGIS: What is it? Hmmm, hmm, interesting!

UNCLE: (*Snatches it back.*) Give it back, not that, this

GENGIS: Oh

UNCLE: Go on, read

GENGIS: I can't, it's all...

UNCLE: Yes?

GENGIS: It's

UNCLE: Well?

GENGIS: Mamman told me never to.

AUNTY: Shall we dance, I've brought my spinning top, it whistles the fandango

GENGIS: Doesn't it know any proper tunes?

UNCLE: Like what? Like the pasa double I suppose, like the old rhumbaba

GENGIS: I know let's rape uncle

AUNTY: Good boy, that's more like it. I must say, I was beginning to think you were a bit of a poof

They seize UNCLE and force her into the bending over position, from there lifting up UNCLE's raincoat the great Khan goes about his business, but after a few moments he stops short.

GENGIS: Hmm this is not buggery as I knew it. Uncle is a woman

AUNTY: That's right, but your little Aunty is a man. Take me I'm yours

GENGIS: You're not yours to give away like that. As regent I insist that you save yourself, have some modesty. This is a kingdom of losers, I want winners. The world will beg for our favours

UNCLE: (*Adjusting his vest.*) We must be patient

GENGIS: We'll enchant them. Death to the collaborator. Death to the traitors. Death to everyone!

AUNTY: Darling

GENGIS: Yes?

AUNTY: There are rumours of a plot against you

GENGIS: What boldness. Who would be so cruel?

AUNTY *and*UNCLE: It's definitely no-one WE know

GENGIS: What happens if they succeed?

AUNTY:	UNCLE:
All that has been gained will be lost	All that has been lost will be gained

GENGIS: How can we refuse?

UNCLE: Politely at first

GENGIS: And if they persist?

UNCLE: Then we'll expose them to the people for the overdressed fascist goons they really are

GENGIS: What if my people are attracted by their gaudy effects? You know what pigs they are, living in squalor and ignorance. What if they made demands on the royal purse?

UNCLE: We shall be ironic with them

GENGIS: Excellent! What if they are ironic back?

UNCLE: Then we shall be sarcastic

GENGIS: Good. And if they are sarcastic too?

UNCLE: Then we shall become absurd

GENGIS: But –

UNCLE: Yes?

GENGIS: What if they are absurd back?

UNCLE: Then we shall be sexy

GENGIS: Sexy? You mean kiss them?

UNCLE: Perhaps

GENGIS: On the lips? Is that what they call democracy?

UNCLE: Yes (*Crosses himself.*)

GENGIS: But they eat tinned fish, don't they? They smell like a cat's fart

UNCLE: We must try to be nimble. We must love them. As they love us

GENGIS: But uncle, they love me most don't they?

UNCLE: They idolise you

GENGIS: Then it's me they'll want to kiss, who knows, maybe more? You know what a kiss can lead to, you know what a vast population we have

UNCLE: Erm. alas no more

GENGIS: No?

UNCLE: No. There was a little accident. Most of them died

GENGIS: Oh. How many left?

UNCLE: Oh loads. Enough anyway to please Your Majesty

AUNTY: Oh definitely

UNCLE: But not enough to leave you ragged

AUNTY: ... no, no not enough for that

GENGIS: Well, that's a relief. You know, Aunty, Uncle, I'm beginning to feel a great warmth welling up, an affection for myself that wasn't there before. I realise that I am the focus of people's hopes and dreams and that through me many destinies will rise or fall; if I block the roads and torch the harvest, millions will suffer

UNCLE: Several will certainly be very upset indeed

GENGIS: Alright, what's next?

UNCLE: Dickwits, the poet laureate is rustling his leaves outside, Your Majesty

GENGIS: At last some uplift after the drudgery of affairs of state. Drag him in

DICKWITS is thrown onto the stage.

DICKWITS: A poem Sire on the occasion of our nation's umpteenth birthday

GENGIS: Good, fire away

DICKWITS: I would like first to say a few words about the nature of poetry, the dialectic between culture and society, between society and the economy, the economy and its corollary, between the corollary and the anomaly, the anomaly and its astronomy, physiognomy and ignominy, ignominy and chim-chiminy, chim-chiminy and tyranny, tyranny and –

GENGIS: Get on with it

DICKWITS: Where to start, where to start indeed.
We started I think appositely in a bus shelter in Hammersmith where we were able to encourage the twenty drivers and conductors –

GENGIS: The poem man!

DICKWITS: Why do we suffer so
                   I don't know

GENGIS: Very neat. Is there more? It's a little flat

DICKWITS: Oh it twists and it turns

GENGIS: Twist away

DICKWITS: I think I know, said a boy
                   Said a boy

GENGIS: Mm

DICKWITS: A change of pace there

GENGIS: Is it likely to change again? I'm getting lost

DICKWITS: I think I know said a boy
                   It's our master's fault

GENGIS: What nonsense! I demand a rewrite

DICKWITS: That's only the first draft. I have something
else already going around in my head. It goes instead
like this
                   I think I know said a boy
                   It's somebody else's fault

GENGIS: That's better. But it's dull

DICKWITS: Dull? I think you will find that it makes
people sit up straight when they hear it

GENGIS: If I want someone to sit up straight I'll put a
railing up their arse

DICKWITS: Of course Your Majesty

GENGIS: And not before

DICKWITS: Quite

GENGIS: Aunty, tell me if I'm wrong but the poetry in
this nation is lard dripping from an old man's chin on
a Sunday afternoon after his dinner

AUNTY: Of course Your Majesty is correct

GENGIS: It's dreary piss on a wall. It's the splatter of
shit from a fat nurse's bum who eats but cannot digest.
All over the toilet bowl, then she neatly wipes it away
because she's embarrassed

AUNTY: Your analysis is unfaltering

GENGIS: But she can't reach all of it

AUNTY: Yes!

GENGIS: Then she glares at you when she meets you on the communal stairway as if you've done her an injury, just because your shoes are muddy

UNCLE: I know the type

GENGIS: And leaving clay on the hallway carpet that's no more than a piece of card to hide the boards

AUNTY: Oh yes indeed!

GENGIS: The boards that are probably stained with her liquid shit, and she hates you because you see it and she's Miss fucking prim and proper

AUNTY: Holier than thou

UNCLE: Nose in the air

GENGIS: Smug and vicious, peeping from behind her curtain "look at him, look at her" but she's worse than the whole blooming lot of them

UNCLE: Squatting over her dinner plate on the floor to try to give it some flavour

AUNTY: Some bloody hopes

GENGIS: No bloody chance of that

AUNTY: Bloody snob

UNCLE: Miss Perfect

GENGIS: The tightest bloody fanny in Finsbury Park

Pause. He muses.

Sad actually, and that's art in this bloody country

UNCLE: You see how it upsets him. What are you going to do about it?

DICKWITS: I shall... involve the community

GENGIS: The what??? You nincompoop. I will not have the royal poet crawling to a selection of brewers belches. And another thing

Tense expectation.

These bus drivers. Louts. And they don't give a tinker's casserole for your poetry. What they want is dancing, and dancing is what you shall provide. Aunty, supply the laureate with bells and let him get on with it

UNCLE: Come on you, out of it

GENGIS: How I enjoy a debate. I told him I think didn't I?

AUNTY: You have single-handedly revolutionised the written word. Would you like us to –

GENGIS: No, he may want to buy something

UNCLE: There is a superfluity of bastards in the realm Sire

GENGIS: And none more superfluous than Dickwits

UNCLE: No My Lord, little babies growing up without that most ceremonious of blessings, a loving father

GENGIS: Gads, we must find these loving fathers and reunite them

UNCLE: They have buggered orf Sire

GENGIS: And left the little babbies? Swines. Let them stay away I say, better off without them

UNCLE: There is the little matter of the expense Sire, falling on the state

GENGIS: Expense? Scandalous. Chop off their heads!

UNCLE: The bastards My Lord?

GENGIS: Bastards louts sluts, all just baggage

UNCLE: Shouldn't we try to force the little families to stay together in their little hovels where they belong?

GENGIS: That's it, Home Sweet Home, by God in my day we stuck it out, kitchen knives, fingers in plug sockets, suicide pills, ambulance, police whatever it took

UNCLE: I shall tell them O great king

GENGIS: Tell who?

UNCLE: The congregation of 257 sluts with babies that is gathered by the royal drawbridge. They claim you are the father

GENGIS: That's impossible. Tell them I am promised to another. I'm sorry but I have a mortgage to think about. And it wasn't me

UNCLE: They each claim knowledge of a mole on your left buttock

GENGIS: There, proof! If I were the father I would hardly have had my back to them, now would I?

UNCLE: I shall tell them

GENGIS: And lest they say I am neglectful of a man's duties tell them I shall build a monument to our passions in the shape of a great tower

UNCLE: Marvelous idea. And what shall this edifice be called?

GENGIS: Borstal

*   *   *

UNCLE: The refugees from Turkeytown have arrived Your Reverence

GENGIS: OK, throw them on the heap

UNCLE: At once. They told me to pass on their thanks in
advance for the jobs

GENGIS: Ha ha ha

UNCLE: And the nice homes

GENGIS: He he he

UNCLE: Which they say are in such short supply
in the war-torn desert they come from

GENGIS: Uncle, I have noticed that the people from this
particular part of Turkeytown are unusually unattractive

UNCLE: Yes Your Majesty

GENGIS: Why is that?

UNCLE: This flank of Turkeytown is famous for its
inbreeding

GENGIS: I see. You know what they need in my opinion, in
order to make them beautiful like us?

UNCLE: Yes?

GENGIS: Immigration

UNCLE: I shall arrange it immediately. Shall I round up
the scum from the tower blocks and send them? Then
these fellows can have their homes

GENGIS: No, send the tarts who lounge around in the city
hotels with their snotty children at government expense,
it will save more money

UNCLE: And where will we put our exotic friends from the
plains of Turkeytown with their multicolored blankets
and their handmade folk sandals?

GENGIS: We shall put them in the hotels

UNCLE: Brilliant

GENGIS: You see something tells me they will enjoy the fluorescent lighting in the bedrooms. The modernity of it will impress them. I can see it now, their children's dark little faces pressed up against the cheap double glazing marveling at the well ordered business of our streets

UNCLE: Ah yes, that reminds me, a study has revealed they have no toys, the little loves

AUNTY: Aah what a shame!

GENGIS: Then send them my broken plastic launching rockets that aunty has trodden on. Give their imaginations something to dwell on

UNCLE: I think they're going to be very happy here. Wait till I get them to school, I have a brilliant plan

GENGIS: Oh yes, they will start off by singing Humpty Dumpty I hope, it's my favourite

UNCLE: No, no sire, not that. You see they won't be able to speak English

GENGIS: Then we shall get them to sing to us in Turkeytownese

UNCLE: No, unfortunately they won't have mastered that either

GENGIS: Surely that is the language their mummies speak to them

UNCLE: No, no, Sire, they speak to them in English

GENGIS: Oh, good

UNCLE: Not *so* good

GENGIS: Why?

UNCLE: Because their mummies can't speak English

GENGIS: Then these poor infants will have no language at all

UNCLE: They will have two broken languages, the advantage being that they are unable to form thoughts in their heads, which makes them perfect material for our education system

GENGIS: Aha! I see, we shall mould them right from the start. Imbue them with the culture of their new country

UNCLE: Oh no Sire that would be horrid! Humpty Dumpty may be alright for you and me, and for any royal children God may grace you with (*Bows gracefully.*) but it is entirely unsuitable for this crew

GENGIS: Oh, why?

UNCLE: It's English. They are foreign. It will make them feel inferior

GENGIS: Naturally

UNCLE: It's our worst fear

GENGIS: What about God then? and Jesus, you know how he wants them for a sunbeam

UNCLE: God and Jesus are English I'm afraid. These foreigners wouldn't grasp it

GENGIS: What shall we teach them then?

UNCLE: We shall teach them their own culture

GENGIS: But we don't know anything about it

UNCLE: Precisely, so we shall make a mish mash of foreign cultures and teach that. It will be entirely neutral, the kiddies won't notice a thing, it will wash over them leaving them... well, numb in a painless sort of a way

GENGIS: What about our own little sunbeams?

UNCLE: You mean the white trash from the estates? They will be relieved of the terrible burden of identity and be left just as confused as the little Turkeytowners. They'll all be in the same boat

GENGIS: Sounds like a recipe for harmony

UNCLE: I like to think so

*   *   *

UNCLE and AUNTY pulling the Khan in a troika.

GENGIS: Who do you think loves the people most, you and aunty, or me?

UNCLE: We love them in different ways

GENGIS: Tell me about the way you love them uncle

UNCLE: I love them because I know them, I share their toils and their burdens

GENGIS: I love them because I don't know them and don't share their toils and their burdens

UNCLE: I love them because they have a wise nobility

GENGIS: I love them because they don't

UNCLE: I love them because they are generous

GENGIS: I love them because I am generous

UNCLE: I love them because they are like abandoned children

GENGIS: I love them because I have abandoned them

UNCLE: I love them –

GENGIS: And I abandoned them because they are so ugly

UNCLE: I love them because through my love they will grow in body and mind and spirit

GENGIS: I love them because they will always remain the pigs that they are

UNCLE: I love them because one day they will be like me

GENGIS: I love them in case one day I should become like them

UNCLE: I love them and one day they will say to me "guide us, show us the way towards the light of universal well-being"

GENGIS: I love them and one day they roll me in the gutter I will look up at their contorted faces and say, "so this is how you repay my love, you dogs"

UNCLE: I –

GENGIS: "How I've suffered for you, how vile and ridiculous I have made myself on your behalfs. Have I not suffered the opprobrium of making your vicious, wretched voice my own. Have I not built glorious imperial towers out of your baseness so high and exalted you have no chance of seeing them, you squinting low-life barenosed scum? Have I not rubbed my hands in your smell and said to the assembled royal banquet "smell this you toffee nosed, half arsed moneygrubbing hypocrites" Have I not as king stood on the table and lifted my skirts and shown myself to the most respected princes and queens out of utter contempt FOR THE WAITERS? Am I not a parvenu, johnnycomelately bacon chewing tyrant all so that on this day, in this your gutter, in this cesspit of yours I could look up at your raised hobnail and say "go on stamp you monsters, but you'd be just like me if you had the balls and the brains and the great love for you all that I have!"

UNCLE: And what would they respond?

GENGIS: They'd take my wallet, and let's be fair, it would be their right

UNCLE: Your generosity is truly regal

GENGIS: They'd have a right to my wallet because it would be empty, and an empty wallet belongs to everyman. And how do you love them Aunty?

AUNTY: I cannot love them because they, sadly, are not worthy my love, but I do fear them, I do admire them, I do... want them

GENGIS: And what do you want them for Aunty?

AUNTY: I want them for so many things. There is a nice girlie brushes my hair and cuts my nails, and a big big man who mends my doggie when she falls over and a tiny tiny woman who clears my toilet when it blocks and they are all three so delicious I could eat them and where would I be without them... but they are not us are they, and we are not them because they beat their children and make their wives do the washing up and say all the wrong things whereas we are nice

GENGIS: Aunty has a point, our people are not nice, they are greedy and mean

AUNTY: They think only of money, they are racists sexists and imperialists

GENGIS: Yes, where do they get it all from?

Pause for thought.

UNCLE: If there's one thing I can't stand it's intolerance

AUNTY: Don't say that word

GENGIS: Intolerance?

AUNTY: I shall scream

GENGIS: You're right aunty, we shall only permit harmony. We shall say to them, live as equals, give what little you have to your brother in need, and he shall be very grateful however small the gift, just as he is grateful for the little we give. If a man comes to you from afar speaking a strange tongue and is in need for he is an eternal pilgrim to our state for his own nation has for centuries been plundered and pillaged, then give him your home, be it ever so small and ramshackle and damp and cheaply built and horrible and ugly, for this man is in need and cannot afford anything better. For you will see in this that you have much in common. And if another man comes to your slum and says behold I am without a home, then give him your son's home or your daughter's home be they ever so humble and windswept and destitute of natural beauty except for the cheer you have brought to it with what's left of your contemptible dying out culture of cockles and mussels and inferior brands. Give this I say to your brother and though it may fall apart in his hands because it is not what he wants or deserves it is nevertheless more than you deserve; and do it not with sour words or fallen countenance, but with the correct words and bright smiles, for be warned that if you do not do it to the utmost, even though your joys are so depleted that you have nothing left to give except that which you no longer possess, if, I say, you do not do this, then it will be said that you are evil and the enemy of mankind

UNCLE: Quite right

GENGIS: I know what I should say if one of these foreign tongued johnnies came to my door asking for my big house

UNCLE: What is that O mighty regent?

GENGIS: Piss off back to the slum you come from

UNCLE: Of course

GENGIS: And if he didn't and insisted on taking up
residence, I should move

UNCLE: Quite right

GENGIS: I can't live in an area full of people like that.
I might be mugged or raped and you can't get real coffee

UNCLE: It's all just a matter of taste. We don't like ghettoes
and slums

AUNTY: Some do, some don't

GENGIS: And quite apart from that, who'd want to live
next door to a load of racist, sexist, imperialists

ALL THREE: Not us

PART II.

UNCLE: Your majesty I have been watching the progress of
the royal policy

GENGIS: Which one?

UNCLE: That of equity for all, fairness, lies, deceit, the
abolition of words and a lot of money for your majesty

GENGIS: Yes

UNCLE: And I have observed its absolute success

GENGIS: Are my people happy?

UNCLE: There is a rosy glow about them to be sure, (*Aside.*)
on their little bottoms

GENGIS: Good. Then it is time for phase two

UNCLE: What is that?

GENGIS: A lock out, a block out, an eclipse of the sun and
moon, drown their pets, bring me their women

UNCLE: Most prudent

GENGIS: Uncle

UNCLE: Yes Matty

GENGIS: Who are these people... My Subjects

UNCLE: A most unworthy bunch. One of them is a dentist, several million do nothing at all, another is a kind of... housing officer

GENGIS: ... Hmm that last one, bring her to me

UNCLE: She cannot be moved. The whole economy would grind to a halt

GENGIS: Then we shall go to her. Where does she live?

UNCLE: In the house Your Majesty

GENGIS: *The* house. Is there but one?

UNCLE: For the moment sire. Building is underway

GENGIS: But where do the rest of my people live?

UNCLE: In *your* house gracious lord

GENGIS: What if I want to sell?

UNCLE: Eviction is a top priority. Eviction and cleanliness make a nation great

GENGIS: Let them all appear before me then

UNCLE: They are... a little shy

GENGIS: Surely in a group they feel confident

UNCLE: They are shy and... a little ill

GENGIS: How ill?

UNCLE: Some poor souls are limbless, some headless, some bodiless

GENGIS: What bold disease has wrecked my population

UNCLE: The disease of being too cocky by half, *and* not knowing the answer to a few simple questions

GENGIS: Is there no cure?

UNCLE: We sent a team of... doctors in

GENGIS: The result?

UNCLE: We're still counting

GENGIS: Well are there any hands or feet that you could bring me I must remain on familiar terms with my people you know

UNCLE: I will have Aunty bring a bag at once

GENGIS: Good. This state business has given me an appetite – please fart into my mouth

UNCLE does so.

*   *   *

GENGIS: Steady me aunty, the inspiration is upon me again; I shall grant freedoms never before dreamt of. I shall make everything illegal

AUNTY: The opposition your majesty...

GENGIS: Don't mention them. They have no poetry in their souls, no philosophy, their arguments are based on a dilated fundament, they sit down too long in the draught and now they blame me. Withdraw their prescriptions!

AUNTY: Quick your majesty, a decree!

GENGIS: Open the prisons!

AUNTY: Your Majesty?

GENGIS: Close the prisons

AUNTY: ?

GENGIS: Open them. Close them. Open them. Close them. Who can tell which is which?

UNCLE: That is a paradox young master

GENGIS: No, it's a dilemma, but not for me. My words come and go with the wind

AUNTY: What a genius. His words have no meaning whatsoever

GENGIS: Oppress the Lowly! Liberate the unloved

AUNTY: Frightening scansion!

GENGIS: What's bad is good, what's good is merely useful, green belt is red tape, red tape is blue ribband... Aunty you are distant today, perhaps it is time once more for the royal bath

Sound of a bath being run.

Come on muckers who will join me?

They strip.

Uncle, what is that legal document in your trousers?

UNCLE: Oh it's nothing, merely wrapping for my member

GENGIS: Please let me see it, take it out

UNCLE: I couldn't

GENGIS: I can see the writing on it from here. Whose names are they? Not your conquests surely

UNCLE: O great king I can conceal it no longer. It is indeed a testimony of loves borne towards me, not conquests though but subjects

GENGIS: My subjects?

UNCLE: It is a petition

GENGIS: It has a formidable length

UNCLE: They say I should snatch the crown from your head, they say the abuses of your regime are... so many they have forgotten them

GENGIS: All of them? Ungrateful wretches! What must a king do?

UNCLE: ... so I drew up a list of them myself

GENGIS: Ah?

UNCLE: They are as follows; you have usurped the role of tyrant which properly belongs to...

GENGIS: Who's he?

UNCLE: Nobody knows. You have spoken only the truth and forbidden fibbing in your cabinet

GENGIS: True

UNCLE: You have forbidden the use of paper. You have fed and clothed the hypocrite and abolished dishonesty

GENGIS: Thank you. I was wondering if anyone had noticed that

UNCLE: You have bragged of your weakness in a most ironical tone

GENGIS: They cheered me for it too God bless 'em

UNCLE: You have pissed on the beach

GENGIS: It pissed on me

UNCLE: Industry has suffered; 100% employment, 1000% productivity, Sales nil

GENGIS: National pride if you'll pardon me uncle. The workers love me for it and I love them

UNCLE: You have housed the homeless

GENGIS: What statesman could do less

UNCLE: In a giant slum

GENGIS: In my own favourite city, in my own arrondissement, in my own house

UNCLE: And charged them exorbitant rents

GENGIS: (*Smiles to himself.*)

UNCLE: And in a swingeing piece of legislative villainy that humiliated the rich and disenfranchised the poor –

GENGIS: Ah the double edged sword!

UNCLE: – You taxed all mention of the underprivileged

GENGIS: What a great burden was thereby lifted from the national vocabulary. A most revealing piece of statecraft

UNCLE: So, with the opposition now withdrawn into self-imposed exile of silence in the capital's northern suburb of H........ you empowered the bootless herd with the right of requisition creating unprecedented shifts of population and a reversal of political allegiances

AUNTY: He is an evil genius

UNCLE: You see sire, they have sinned, you have sinned, we have sinned, I... well I have corrected sin from my blackened soul and am now pure

GENGIS: Forget that now, I have something important to say to my people. (*Goes to his balcony, returns.*) I shall tell them; Lords ladies and gentlemen, forgive yourselves, forgive your brothers and sisters, forgive me, try not... try... have faith. Don't you think that is rather moving?

UNCLE: Yes it is moving. But I would like to move them in some other way

He manipulates his rolled petition with barely controlled ferocity.

Exit.

GENGIS: Aunty, I am afraid. The kingdom once renowned for its modest charms has become a bunker where people perform deeds of darkness upon one another

AUNTY: Oh it's only their way

GENGIS: Their way of what?

AUNTY: Their way of saying (*With great sentimentality.*) "we are people too you know"

GENGIS: Oh I see, and the murdering and torturing that goes on in our parks and woodlands for entertainment?

AUNTY: Oh it's only their little way

GENGIS: Their little way of what?

AUNTY: Their little way of saying "sometimes we're lonely, sometimes we're afraid, sometimes we don't really know what is wrong; so we take someone and we pull their teeth out with pliers, then set fire to them, a little group of chums together, girls and boys, supportive, caring, no nasty words"

GENGIS: What does it all mean aunty?

AUNTY: (*Ferocious.*) It means the devil is amongst us, put the boot in hard while you've still got the chance. Put bars up at your window, don't talk to yourself after 8 pm, don't give an inch or they'll take a mile, string em up, cut them down. You see?

GENGIS: Yes, I see

AUNTY: It's just their little way of saying (*Babytalk.*) We're lost and lost and lost and lost and we don't know our way home. (*More so.*) We want some more money

GENGIS: But wait. *I* want some more money

AUNTY: Don't interrupt. It's their little way of saying, we want free this free that and free the other

GENGIS: Bastards! Wait till I catch them

AUNTY: They want you to be their scapegoat

GENGIS: Do they?

AUNTY: They want to blame you for the piss in their lifts

GENGIS: But I'm a socialist. I would never piss in a lift

AUNTY: Perhaps you haven't explained that well enough. You must communicate

GENGIS: I'll make a play a book a poem

AUNTY: That way they'll all understand. They love plays and books and poems

GENGIS: But how? They're all so thick

AUNTY: We'll put it on television and call it Bingo Wingo Zingo Zam Powee

GENGIS: What if they come round to watch it on my tv set? I'm not having any of them in here, they all stink of air freshener. Do they wear toilet cleaner as perfume?

AUNTY: Yes son they do

GENGIS: Maybe it's too late to help them

AUNTY: Aaah don't say that. Imagine their little faces looking up at you with their big eyes "please help us don't to be such ignorant Tory Goons"

GENGIS: The bigoted swines. The thought of them makes me want not just to piss in their lifts but to shit on their brains

AUNTY: It's been done. They have done it to themselves. Out of sheer bloody-mindedness of course

GENGIS: Ha! So British. So land of hope and glory. So U.K.

AUNTY: Doesn't it make you proud to be not British

GENGIS: Yes, urgh! I'm half Maltese

AUNTY: I'm half Madagascan

GENGIS: I'm half Chinese

AUNTY: I'm half Indonesian

GENGIS: I'm half Polynesian

AUNTY: I'm half Melanesian

GENGIS: I'm half *MALVENIAN*

AUNTY: I'm supporting the African teams in the World cup

GENGIS: I'm supporting India in the alternative World cup

AUNTY: I'm supporting rabbits in the animal World cup

GENGIS: I'm supporting poor little pussies in the World Cup for animals with electrodes in their little brains

AUNTY: I'm supporting animals that aren't in any teams because they are too sick because they've been eaten by doggies in the garden

GENGIS: *You* HYPOCRITE!

AUNTY: ?

GENGIS: You train your dog to kill the very birds in the trees

AUNTY: Only bedause he's hungwy...

GENGIS: Remind me, what is it just their little way of saying?

AUNTY: It's just their little way of saying that when the suffering is all too much it's time to stop for a few moments of reflection, a little sadness fills your heart, you can't go on, a tear comes to your eye, a sob mounts inside your head chest throat your eye, your vision blackens, a whisper from far away says "someone, please if there is anyone, please forgive us"

GENGIS: But, aunty, why don't we all love each other anymore? Has it always been like this?

AUNTY: I hope you don't think I'm old enough to remember?

GENGIS: Sometimes I get so depressed aunty

AUNTY: What you need is something to cheer you up

GENGIS: I know! The assizes! Justice!

AUNTY: That's right. It'll put the colour back in your cheeks

GENGIS: Bring in the first accused

AUNTY: The first accused is... Dickwits

DICKWITS is thrown onto the stage.

GENGIS: Ah Dickwits, you bastard. What have you done to my people? You have ravaged them haven't you with your horrible claustrophobia. You've tried to hypnotise them but they didn't want you did they, they didn't fancy it. Well serve you right. They've turfed you out haven't they, but not before you degraded their palettes, they were gourmets once now they drink vinegar, even the babies. This is all down to your moral rectitude which you keep inviting everyone to examine. Well you've bent over once too often Dickwits, you've smiled sideways at

the camera for the last time, you promised so much
and delivered so little, you're on your way to the awards
ceremony in the sky, see what the cherubim make of
your inauguration speech and while you're at it you can
cast my vote for me in the general election, then we'll
see what you smell like when you're laughing on the
other side of your face, counting your onions in your
rotten borough. You think I don't know, you think
I don't care, well look at these – real tears! Real tears
mark you, not bought with your socialist shilling, not
banged out on your Country Life anvil either, none of
your cold steel here Charlie I can assure you, none of
your street carnivals and residents committees where
I come from, we didn't submit it to a panel in my
comprehensive mate; playing fields? what bloomin'
playing fields? Just turn the page and read on. You're
plain Jane, Dicky boy, you're drab, right down to your
wife's bangles and your beads and your patent leather
shoes and your aerosol can. You've tidied up a bit too
much is all I can say, you've hoovered my favourite
tree and strangled that little Dicky bird with your
endless bloody explanations. You want a goal for
tomorrow, I know you do my fair-weather friend, you
may not recognise this court my fine fellow but we saw
you coming a mile off so there's no use in shrugging your
shoulders you're in there somewhere, by Christmas! You
won't be sitting on that wall for long with this morning's
egg on your face, don't worry about that, because you've
been bought. Oh didn't you think you were a retail item?
Retail? Retail. You're in the bloody clearance sale mate,
you were *never* full price, you can call it priceless if you
want but I know what your posh customers call it on
their way home behind your back. You don't know what
I'm referring to do you, you don't know what I mean?
It's all Greek to you isn't it Charlie until you're sick
of hearing it. Well, have you ever wondered why? Help

me down from here, I'm ready for my operation. You
perform it Dicky boy, because I know you mean well
and I'm grateful. I trust you, more than I'd trust a friend.
Bless you darling. OK doctor I'm ready, get your cross-
saws out

UNCLE has returned with the necessary equipment.

Trepanning begins.

UNCLE: You see Dicky boy how you have won the royal
favour? He skirted around it now but there's no denying
how your muscular verse style and poetic diction has
made a deep impression on his temporal lobe. This
could be your opportunity to jog his memory

DICKWITS saws assiduously.

GENGIS: (*Speaking from the operating table.*) You can't hide it
from me any longer, I have no kingdom left do I?

UNCLE: Well, no...

GENGIS: What darkness is this, what sadness fills the
world? What have I done?

UNCLE: One or two misjudged policies

GENGIS: Tell me, wasn't I radical enough?

UNCLE: Radical? You have chopped down to the roots and
laid them bare

AUNTY: The whole kingdom goes about without a stitch of
clothing on its back. Not a fault is hidden

UNCLE: Our wounds, all our sores

AUNTY: ... our blisters

UNCLE: ... our broken limbs

AUNTY: ... our torn eyelids, open beside the ditches

UNCLE: the whole nation groans. There's no talk of a lack of radicalism

AUNTY: No-one says if only he were

UNCLE: ... more

AUNTY: ... radical

UNCLE: No-one

AUNTY: ... for they cannot speak

UNCLE: Not a man among them can utter a word

AUNTY: ... enough to say –

UNCLE: ... more radical please

AUNTY: No worry on that score

GENGIS: I don't know then.

Pause.

... perhaps I wasn't moderate enough

AUNTY: Of course you were. You have been moderate.. in moderation

UNCLE: When it suits. Have you ever wanted to be moderate and not been?

GENGIS: No

UNCLE: There then moderate with a free will

AUNTY: Randomly moderate with a free hand

UNCLE: You have dispensed moderation with liberality, with a glad hand

AUNTY: Generously giving it away like gifts to your friends

UNCLE: Here friend, aunt, uncle, here is a moderate gift,
a gift given in moderation

Sawing continues, UNCLE slips out.

GENGIS: Aunty, what is life all about?

AUNTY: That, nephew, is one of life's little mysteries

GENGIS: When will the mystery be solved?

AUNTY: Just before it's all over, when you will realise
in the words of Dickwits here our national bard "all
is vanity" In the face of death you will suddenly come
over all sick and all scared and the allure of vain projects
will pass away; Your books – you were never to read
them, Your beautiful home – you were never to live in
it, Your beautiful wife is a failure, Your favourite side of
bacon in the pantry – covered in bile. It will all disappear

GENGIS: How do you know this aunty?

AUNTY: (*Whispers to him.*)

GENGIS: Is that why you so often smile secretly to
yourself in that strange way?

AUNTY: (*Does so.*) Perhaps

GENGIS: I am pleased you have revealed these things
to me, aunty, for I am now glad that this nation has been
relieved of its its its –

AUNTY: It's...

GENGIS: ... well everything

AUNTY: Yes

GENGIS: It is a good thing for the people because they are
closer now to the meaning of life as revealed in the last
moments of bitter painful nausea you described so well

AUNTY: Thank you

GENGIS: Keep a nation close to death and they will be
close to life

AUNTY: Yes, that is true. True words son. True, true words

GENGIS: Unfortunately I don't think my people have
benefited from the terrible knowledge available to them

AUNTY: Why not?

GENGIS: Because they are all watching tv

AUNTY: Bless them

GENGIS: What is that clumping bumping sound?

AUNTY: That musical marching?

GENGIS: Yes that clomping and stomping

AUNTY: That clippity cloppity?

GENGIS: Yes that munching and crunching

AUNTY: That hippity boppity?

GENGIS: Yes that gnashing and grinding

AUNTY: That skippity hoppity?

GENGIS: Yes, that horrible noise!

AUNTY: That's your uncle on his horse

GENGIS: He must make a fine figure of a man. Aunty
I have begun to notice a sublime look upon Uncle's
face. Perhaps he has discovered this enlightenment
you speak of? And just now, well it must have been
an apparition...

AUNTY: Dreamy boy what did you see?

GENGIS: Uncle, in a small room with what appeared to
be... friends

AUNTY: One of his workshops

GENGIS: They were waving their arms in the air

AUNTY: Just a warm up dearie to prevent it all becoming too headbound

GENGIS: And when I asked what they were doing they turned at once and looked at me with strange hollow eyes

AUNTY: They were probably just tired Gengis darling, your uncle is a terrible bore when he's helping people express themselves

GENGIS: But aunty, there was a strange sense of evil in the room

UNCLE bursts in.

UNCLE: Yes and what's wrong with that you little squealer

GENGIS: But uncle you were always so loving and caring

UNCLE: Yes, and I shall love my people all the more once they have achieved the perfection I have planned for them

GENGIS: It sounds wonderful. And what kind of perfection do you have in mind?

UNCLE: In my dream kingdom supplicants line the streets. They fling money at you as you pass by, they lurk in every shop doorway and you are expected to hurl insults at them in return

GENGIS: Is it easy to think of any?

UNCLE: I usually cry out things like; nit-pickers! slow brains! limping fellows! ant-teasers! Operatives! rotten vest!

GENGIS: Are they pleased with these?

UNCLE: I mention only a few of their favourites. I shall give animus to the pusillanimous, I shall make the crooked straight, where there is doubt I shall bring certainty, I shall never surrender

GENGIS: How will you do all this uncle?

UNCLE: Words

GENGIS: Aha

UNCLE: Yes it's all a matter of finding the right words

GENGIS: And if that doesn't work?

UNCLE: Then I have this big knobbledy stick

GENGIS: Then you are bound to succeed. We are looking forward to the new order aren't we aunty?

AUNTY: Yes dear

GENGIS: But uncle, those strange leather boots

UNCLE: Inside the top of my boots I have frogs for my enemies

AUNTY: Urgh!

UNCLE: Beware the man who denies my people the right to be very happy indeed

GENGIS: Beware indeed

UNCLE: Nothing but the best for my boys

AUNTY: Quite right

UNCLE: The quest awaits me

GENGIS: And will you bring back food to feed the hungry babies?

UNCLE: Better than that. I shall return at the head of a dark-browed column of the red-trimmed sons of judgement

AUNTY: How thrilling and chilling

GENGIS: But uncle I'm afraid, I like things as they are. I like being Gengis Khan, I like being the people's choice, I like taking everyone's money uncle, I like eating my little bowl of mumsmilk yoghurt of an evening, I like cheating in the elections and tricking the people and I like reading pornography in the bath, please don't spoil it

UNCLE: Call that destiny, you money grubbing degenerate, you low minded sensualist pervert you? – (*Farts loudly.*)

GENGIS: Uncle, you have farted

UNCLE: Yes and let that be a warning to you. I shall expel all unnatural gases from the temple of my rectum until the whole of Europe stinks of my evacuation. I shall be free and you my lad will cough your Jewish lungs onto the table

GENGIS: (*Does so.*)

Does this mean no World Cup?

UNCLE: There will be one but my team will win or several million will live to regret it

The dog barks at him.

Tell that thing to shut up

AUNTY: I can't sweetie he's excited by the noisome cloud still clinging to your slacks

UNCLE: Then I shall silence his indignity (*He stamps on the puppy's neck rendering it silent.*)

AUNTY: Oh brute, brute, poor little doggie! You wicked man, you cruel man!

UNCLE marches out.

AUNTY: What a terrible change. Do you think we should have his throat cut to preserve world peace?

GENGIS: No, he may want to buy something

AUNTY: Sing us some gentle songs of suffering

GENGIS: I've trained long and hard for this. Quick tie me up, lower me down, into the royal casket, this is no head cold. Don't you recognise the Imperial goitre when you see it?

AUNTY: Uncle! the razor sharp incisions of our national poet have finally brought the tyrant to his last breath. Come back quick!

UNCLE: (*Enters.*) Incredible. But shall the nation be denied one last goodbye?

GENGIS: Alright, file them past but make it quick, the royal memories are washing over my consciousness. Gee whiz uncle, I was truly a pippin!

UNCLE: Bien sûr

GENGIS: Who are these people aunty?

AUNTY: They are your subjects

GENGIS: O their breaths are certainly no sweeter than when I came to the throne. Has it really all been in vain? Fuck damn my own stupid head for thinking up this idea, but I'll stick to it anyway. It will improve, where is Dickwits?

DICKWITS: I'm sorry Your Highness, you were trepanned in good faith

GENGIS: What part of my brain did they remove?

DICKWITS: Your judgment Sire. And you'll find your backhand in tennis a good deal worse

GENGIS: My way with women is intact I see

A worthy erection protrudes the blanket.

DICKWITS: Ah the hangman's cudgel, as we call it Your Majesty

GENGIS: Dicky, forgive me if I have been glib with you. I love you

DICKWITS: You're fading fast Your Majesty. Should I pen a dying speech for you, your last words?

GENGIS: Not on your life Dicky boy, even a farting corpse is more eloquent than the squeaking of your pips Thanks but no thanks

DICKWITS bows and exits backwards.

GENGIS: You wait. Indira will come back one day and you'll see. All this piffle-paffle, all this... politics! Indira is beautiful, Indira is full of love, Indira has a temple of humanity in her breast, Indira has long black hair and smooth feet, and they are walking this way I can sense it

AUNTY: And what do you think she'll make of you?

GENGIS: She loves the people and they love her, she IS the people. She is me. I am her. I am the people. I love her. I love the people. I love myself

UNCLE: It's all very well to come out with all this now I must say. We haven't noticed you being very loving, have we?

AUNTY: No

UNCLE: We haven't noticed you kissing little babies and having a joke with the pensioners. You're not exactly an antivivisectionist are you, not exactly a vegan, not exactly a supporter of freedom fighters on the street corners on a Saturday morning with a bucket and a newspaper are you?

GENGIS: I'm anti abortion

AUNTY: You papist!

GENGIS: Aha, so you'd like me to persecute Catholics now?

UNCLE: *Not* if they're Irish and wave the tricolour

GENGIS: Damned if I can keep track of it

UNCLE: Your frivolous attitude reduces politics to mere flibber flabber, blibby blabby, gibber gabber

GENGIS: It's your fault, you keep moving the goal posts

UNCLE: Gengis, don't worry, just do as we do, say what we say, we'll keep an eye on you

GENGIS: Thanks uncle. I do try

UNCLE: Alright good boy. His heart is in the right place

AUNTY: It's all over the bloody place. What he needs is a good kick in the cunt!

UNCLE: Alright aunty, we shall kick him there if he does it again

AUNTY: Hear? So just watch it

UNCLE: Isn't it sad to see a noble man sunk so low

AUNTY: And all because he tried to steal the march on his neighbour

UNCLE: But what a neighbour. People are saying he was not a man of total frankness regarding his relations with Indira

AUNTY: What treachery. So it was all a mirage

UNCLE: Remember how he went bankrupt soon after Indira left, and he shut up shop and disappeared? It transpires they were seen naked together on the banks of a river

AUNTY: And this is the sad eyed goddess who so castigated poor Gengis for his little retailing peccadillo!

UNCLE: The very same, laughing in the moonlight with the sperm of her husband's rival swimming in her beautiful brown belly... So they say

GENGIS: When Indira comes I shall not ask her where she's been. Perhaps on her arrival she will give birth to the child of a fornicator and that child I shall wrap up in my arms and take it out and show my people; behold your deliverer! I shall call out to them, and they shall cry tears of joy

* * *

Day. Dawn. Night. Twilight. Day. Dawn. Night. Dawn. Twilight. Dawn. Day. Night.

GENGIS: Stop that

AUNTY: Well, what's next Plucky?

GENGIS: I shall merge the VD and cancer clinics. Better atmosphere and save money

UNCLE: Getting a little nervous about the approach of your beloved?

GENGIS: She loves me uncle. She loves me. She loves me. ME. She loves me. ME ME ME

UNCLE: If indeed she has the roving eye your days are surely numbered. You'd better get out quick in a getaway car

GENGIS: Will you drive in that case uncle?

UNCLE: Sorry son, cramp in my right hand, lassitude of my left

GENGIS: Aunty darling, we'll drive off together. We'll stop off and get some shopping

AUNTY: Can we can we can we really?

GENGIS: Yes alright

AUNTY: In my favourite mall, in my favourite shopping centre. I love the fountains, soft stream of light

GENGIS: That's right aunty

AUNTY: No fucking riff raff there

GENGIS: No

AUNTY: Just shoppers, shopping shopping shopping shopping shopping shopping shopping shopping shopping

GENGIS: Buying toys at Christmas most of them

AUNTY: Yippee

GENGIS: Big new duvets and sideboards

AUNTY: Oooo

GENGIS: Holidays

AUNTY: Yippee

GENGIS: Watches

AUNTY: Watches!

GENGIS: Lovely shoppers aunty, all waiting for you to come and join in

AUNTY: Yippee

GENGIS: Boom and bust boom and bust

AUNTY: Yippee

GENGIS: But watch out aunty, keep your hands to yourself

AUNTY: Alright but if any police get in my way I'll fucking run them down

GENGIS: Alright, that's ok

AUNTY: I'll fucking go window shopping with them on the bumper

GENGIS: (*Sudden tears.*) It's no good I love her, I love her, I want my baby

UNCLE: But she doesn't want you. Not since the days of the old shoponthecorner have you heard so much as a postcard. You see she has become interested in world affairs

GENGIS: What? You mean she watches the news?

UNCLE: Yes

GENGIS: Then... she's well informed

UNCLE: Yes

GENGIS: She knows what's going on?

UNCLE: Yes she does and she reads the newspapers listens to the radio and looks at pictures, she's plugged in, she's got your number

GENGIS: Bitch. I hate women like that

UNCLE: You can't argue with progress

GENGIS: They glance at Titbits and they think they're Bertolucci

UNCLE: I know

GENGIS: Ignorance is the bane of our age

Very long pause.

GENGIS: Most people are too dumb to realise that

AUNTY: Ready sonny?

GENGIS: It's no good, I can't go. Without her I am nothing

AUNTY: She'll chop your little head off

GENGIS: But first I shall taste the sweet sorrow of her
rebuke, It is enough

UNCLE: Then you will have to watch while I supply her
with all the evidence against you

GENGIS: Of course good kind uncle. You are a man
of high ideals for which no sacrifice is too great, no
treachery too low. I understand

UNCLE: That's correct my boy. You shall be an egg in my
omelette

GENGIS: I shan't protest. If she says I was ambitious
I shall say I am a man, if she says I was cruel, I shall
say I loved only justice, if she says I was rash I shall
say I am a poet at heart, if she says I was corrupt I shall
say my duty has corrupted me, if she says I lied I shall
say I love the truth too much to speak it, if she says
I stole the lightbulbs I shall show her the palace of lights
I built in her honour, if she says I betrayed my country
I shall say I have no country for I am a child of the
universe and anyone who believed otherwise was a
sucker, if she says I betrayed my class I shall say my
class has produced quite enough heroes for any epoch,
if she says I betrayed my god I shall bless her, if she says
I burnt books I shall show her my poems, if she says
I trampled the blind and mislead the lame, well, I am
no doctor and neither is she, if she says I believe in an
incorrect political analysis, I shall say the analysis
believes me but I believe no-one, if she says I am a
tyrant I shall inform her that in the name of democracy

all my policy decisions were taken by the cleaners, you'd better take it up with them, if she says I buggered aunty's doggie I shall say who can resist that sexy little pet and its waddle, and if she says I have no love I shall crash my cymbals and dance and sing and say YES! Let us speak of love!

UNCLE: Dickwits has made himself visible through the portcullis

GENGIS: What does he want?

UNCLE: He can't say, he's unusually short of wind

GENGIS: You'd better let him in or he'll say I'm playing hard to get

DICKWITS is thrown onto the stage.

Well, what is it?

DICKWITS: The beautiful Indira is coming. She is walking across the desert at the head of a large force

GENGIS: At last. Where are you going uncle?

UNCLE: I'm going to meet her. Coming aunty?

AUNTY: Yes, of course. Lovely girl

GENGIS: It's me she wants

UNCLE: Ok Gengis, one last request, before Indira comes

GENGIS: One last request. Alright. A cigarette. No, two cigarettes. No a cigar

UNCLE: It has been smoked, sorry

GENGIS: Alright then, a meal

UNCLE: The doggie has just eaten it I'm afraid

GENGIS: Anything will do then

UNCLE: Anything at all?

GENGIS: Anything

UNCLE: Name something

GENGIS: A magazine

UNCLE: Neither of us can reach

GENGIS: Get me some money

UNCLE: Money?

GENGIS: Yes! Sell someone something

UNCLE: There's nothing to sell that everyone hasn't
    already got

GENGIS: Get me a merchant

UNCLE: He's in his yacht

GENGIS: Get me an architect

UNCLE: He's in his rectangle

GENGIS: Get me lions and tigers

UNCLE: They are printed in a book

GENGIS: Get me my philosopher

UNCLE: He's crowded in his house

GENGIS: Get me a museum

UNCLE: It's under ground

GENGIS: Get me a park with fountains

UNCLE: We've moved it outside town

GENGIS: Get me an honest man to be my friend

UNCLE: He's on tv

GENGIS: Get me a beautiful girl

UNCLE: She's unable

GENGIS: Get me a smell

UNCLE: It's on your fingers

DICKWITS puts the noose around his neck.

GENGIS: Get me a rope

UNCLE: It's around your neck

GENGIS: Get me a priest

UNCLE: He's singing his song and clapping his hands

GENGIS: Get me a blindfold

UNCLE: It's nowhere to be seen

GENGIS: Get me a tree

UNCLE: There's only two planks

DICKWITS helps him onto a chair.

GENGIS: Get me a chair

UNCLE: You're on it

GENGIS: Get me a pardon

UNCLE gives silver to DICKWITS who exits.

UNCLE: Pardon? Can't hear you

GENGIS: Get the hangman

UNCLE: He's spending his guinea

GENGIS: Get me Indira Indira Indira!

UNCLE: She's right here, just coming

GENGIS: Aunty, why do the men and women have no forgiveness in their hearts?

AUNTY: Because it would burst their little hearts

GENGIS: Aunty, why do their eyes fill with tears?

AUNTY: They're thinking about the tears in their eyes like me what I do when I want to cry

GENGIS: Aunty why do I never win a prize?

AUNTY: Because there is no prize for you

GENGIS: Aunty why does the wind blow?

AUNTY: Because of those nasty weather men

GENGIS: Aunty, why has my tree fallen down?

AUNTY: I cannot tell a lie, you cut it down with your big shiny axe of silver and gold you did you cut it down

GENGIS: Aunty why are we out here in the terrible cold?

AUNTY: Because we are together holding hands

GENGIS: Aunty, why can no-one read the book?

AUNTY: Upsidedowninsideoutbacktofront

GENGIS: Aunty, why the biggest baboon?

AUNTY: Because the kangaroo shoes jump higher

GENGIS: Aunty, why so quiet in the sky?

AUNTY: Because the crows are cawing elsewhere

GENGIS: Aunty why the ragged soldier in his trench

AUNTY: Because the shiny general on his horse

GENGIS: Why the judge upon his bench?

AUNTY: Because the rope around his neck

GENGIS: Aunty, what happens when you plant a seed?

AUNTY: The seed begins to grow

GENGIS: What happens when the seed begins to grow?

AUNTY: The clouds begin to fill with snow

GENGIS: What happens when the snow begins to fall?

AUNTY: The birdie sits upon the wall

GENGIS: What happens when the wall begins to crack?

AUNTY: The stick falls down upon your back

GENGIS: What happens when my back begins to bleed?

AUNTY: Then you are dead and dead indeed

GENGIS: What happens when the cat's away?

AUNTY: The mice begin to play

AUNTY tiptoes off.

GENGIS: Aunty, I'm frightened

GENGIS stands on the chair with the rope around his neck.

The End.

IN PRAISE OF PROGRESS

Characters

MR. BARON

BUBBLES

MR. SMITH

MR. GREENHOUSE

MARVIN

MR. FISCHBEIN

MRS. FISCHBEIN

LITTLE NEIGHBOUR GIRL

MRS. BULIMA

FRIEND

CROWS

1ST MAN

2ND MAN

3RD MAN

4TH MAN

5TH MAN

6TH MAN

7TH MAN

First performed on radio by the BBC, IN PRAISE OF PROGRESS received its first stage production in April 1999 at the Théâtre de l'Odéon, Paris, where it was directed by Lukas Hemleb.

PART ONE

Beside a gentle flowing river.

MR BARON: What are you men doing

1ST MAN: A fish has fallen in the water and we're trying to fish it out

MR BARON: With what are you trying to fish it out?

2ND MAN: With sticks and stones

MR BARON: What kind of fish is this?

2ND MAN: The normal fish, of flesh and bones

MR BARON: What kind of men are you?

3RD MAN: The normal men of blood and stones

MR BARON: Why aren't you back at your jobs to earn your keep

4TH MAN: This is our lunch, this is our way of resting mate, this is our fishing-break, this is how we take it easy and get back what has been lost. I rest my stick upon my gut and cast my stones

MR BARON: How did this fish fall in?

5TH MAN: He didn't fall he was pushed

6TH MAN: But not by us

7TH MAN: We didn't push him in

1ST MAN: We're fishing him out

2ND MAN: We're having a little swim, we're wading in the water and our trousers are wet, and our shoes, we're just normal blokes

3RD MAN: We're neighbours, just the common bunch, he's the neighbour, he's the neighbour, he's the neighbour and he's the neighbour, mate

4TH MAN: The high life is not for us, we prefer a pint. Now if you wouldn't mind, we'd like to be angling here in solitude, now we've given you the benefit of our inner thoughts

5TH MAN: Yes, if you don't mind, we're grieving. This poor fish, this poor little fish that we don't like. It's hard to grieve. But we like to pay our debts. We go to any lengths sometimes. It's only our way, our only way

*   *   *

Beside the river.

MR SMITH: My eyesight is twisted with suspicion

BUBBLES: You've lost your compassion you mean

MR SMITH: Exactly. I thought I had it but it was gone. I kept it hidden to preserve it but it went rancid, it rotted away. I forgot where to find it and in the end I could only find it by the smell

BUBBLES: Alright, that's enough

MR SMITH: The stench, the terrible stink of cruelty. The crueller I am the more compassion was once there and has been lost

BUBBLES: I understand already

MR SMITH: And then, even the cruelty faded away and I became lazy and ignorant, a fountain of bile

BUBBLES: Stop now

MR SMITH: There are scenes between people no-one should ever see

BUBBLES: Then just don't tell anyone

MR SMITH: And one more thing. What if I lost you and couldn't find you?

BUBBLES: Then you would go to my house and find me there. You have no need to worry

MR BARON: (*Approaching, to himself.*) By Jove it's my friend Mr Smith kneeling at the feet of that young woman. I wonder if he saw the catastrophe. Mr Smith! Mr Smith!

BUBBLES: Good bye my love (*Walks away.*)

MR BARON: Did you see the catastrophe Mr Smith, did you see them murdering that poor boy? I saw the riot, I saw them marching up and down, I saw the whole thing, I saw the fear in his eyes when they caught him and hanged him and drowned him

Pause.

Indeed it was a terrible thing

Pause.

A cruel heartless thing to do

Pause.

A cruel heartless thing that ignores the value and uniqueness of a human life

Pause.

You say nothing Mr Smith

MR SMITH: I agree with you but what you say is obvious, Mr Baron

MR BARON: Oh yes, but I always discover that the more I repeat the obvious, the less people believe me, which rather suggests it was not sufficiently obvious in the first place. Are you going after that young woman?

MR SMITH: Yes...

Very long pause.

MR BARON: Well?

MR SMITH: em...

MR BARON: You've nothing to say about anything have you Mr Smith?

MR SMITH: No, nothing

MR BARON: You hope she will inspire you

MR SMITH: Goodbye Mr Baron

*   *   *

BUBBLE's father's house. Middle class.

MR GREENHOUSE: You're very welcome here Mr Smith, my daughter has told us all about you – not happy she says. That's alright with me, neither am I. In my younger days I used to be happy, I once laughed for six months non-stop

MR SMITH: Yes

MR GREENHOUSE: Now you met I hear, on the banks of a river. There is some confusion over what you were doing there. My son swears Bubbles told him you were about to throw yourself in, whereas she insists to me that you were trying to save a man who had been pushed by a mob

MR SMITH: Neither is true. I was there merely because your daughter was there. I did nothing. We stood beside a tree

MR GREENHOUSE: Ah yes, hence the confusion – this was the very tree from which they hanged their victim before drowning him

MR SMITH: No, that is incorrect, this was a tiny little tree.

MR GREENHOUSE: Now my son says you made some
foul and inexplicable comments about the goings on,
also that this is where you first kissed my daughter

MR SMITH: He's wrong, we didn't kiss at all

MR GREENHOUSE: Suffice to say, she brought you
home. Your proposal took us all by surprise

MR SMITH: Did it?

MR GREENHOUSE: Are you damaged goods Mr Smith?
Have you accumulated a lot of personal faults along the
way? Fear it, Mr Smith, fear it. Whatever weakness that
is within you she will find it. She won't do anything to
harm you but just her knowing is painful enough. I'm
her father Mr Smith, but I am a dog, deservedly so
I admit. I have chosen to ignore her. I have a life to
live dammit. She is a Titian, but I enjoy my imitations
of Otto Dix, do you mind?

MR SMITH: No I don't mind

MR GREENHOUSE: My imitations of Paul Klee

MR SMITH: I understand

MR GREENHOUSE: My Barbara Hepworth Sketches

MR SMITH: Yes

MR GREENHOUSE: I do strange lines in blue ink on
pieces of aluminium if I feel like it, Mr Smith. Shall
I tell you why? Because it's all rubbish and it wouldn't
matter even if it weren't, it still wouldn't matter, in the
scheme of things as I'm sure you'll agree. You must have
worked that out by your age

MR SMITH: Yes, I've worked it out

MR GREENHOUSE: It's a question of blood Mr Smith.
How much blood is it worth? I'll tell you, none, nothing
is worth a drop of blood

MR SMITH: Other blood?

MR GREENHOUSE: Other blood. Yes, of course other blood. Of course other blood is worth blood

Pause.

Well that's dampened everything..... You see I like to see myself as no longer a participant. That is my right as a piece of animal flesh born to woman. I picture a field on a hillside, a cow, blood and so on, she has calved me. This, strangely, is the best way I have of remembering I am human, otherwise I am engulfed by the temporary sorrows of mankind. My cow vision inspires me to thought, to feelings. I was beginning to lose sight of myself until... I saw the vision of the calf – the birth of man

MR SMITH: Yes, I see it. I can grasp it. Cows are, after all, cattle

MR GREENHOUSE: If you must, Mr Smith, if you must

*   *   *

In the garden.

BUBBLES: You met my father inside

MR SMITH: Yes, he was telling me something very interesting. He was telling me about his vision of himself as a calf dropped from a cow on a hillside and how this picture for him brings back a sense of his being alive and how from that beginning it is a short step to the superman standing on a mountain top shouting at the sky and preparing to throw himself off into the abyss below. He's a fascinating man, your father, you're not listening.

BUBBLES: No, I'm looking at you and wondering why you're saying this to me

MR SMITH: It's just conversation

BUBBLES: What I mean is: I wonder why you aren't
saying something else

MR SMITH: Because I can't imagine what that something
else could be

Silence.

Well, that was very clever... You've called my bluff.
Now I have to admit that I *would* like a response to
what I said just now

BUBBLES: So it *was* important

MR SMITH: Yes

BUBBLES: I'm sorry then because I really wasn't listening.
If you want to ask me something why don't you simply
ask me

MR SMITH: Ask you? Alright I'll ask you. No. I don't
know what to ask you

BUBBLES: Because you don't want to ask me you want to
attack me

MR SMITH: Yes alright I want to attack you

BUBBLES: That makes me very sad

MR SMITH: I don't see why. So, you'd like me to be nice
to you is that it?

BUBBLES: Why do you keep trying to insult me by
misunderstanding

MR SMITH: I don't. You keep ending the conversation,
I'm trying to keep it going

BUBBLES: This isn't a conversation

MR SMITH: Oh yes it is

BUBBLES: It's not a direct one

MR SMITH: I don't want a direct one I want this one

BUBBLES: Alright

MR SMITH: Go on then answer

BUBBLES: What's the question?

MR SMITH: Every time I ask one you tell me that's not the one I wanted to ask

BUBBLES: We're not getting on are we

MR SMITH: Don't say that! You're so pessimistic that you don't even dare have an argument

BUBBLES: No because the memory of it will make me love you less

MR SMITH: What kind of love is that?

BUBBLES: I don't want you to show me that you don't know me, because then I will stop trusting you

MR SMITH: I see! Can't I just pretend not to know you so we can have the argument

BUBBLES: You must never treat me so lightly

MR SMITH: I need you to listen to me

BUBBLES: Then you must say things I can understand

MR SMITH: You don't mean 'understand'

BUBBLES: No, I mean things I can respect

MR SMITH: Then you consider there was something wrong with what I said in the first place. But you weren't listening

BUBBLES: I couldn't understand it

MR SMITH: Do you mean understand or respect?

BUBBLES: I couldn't understand why you whom I respect
was saying it

MR SMITH: Saying what? What did I say?

BUBBLES: Maybe you weren't listening either. You were
trying to say that just because mankind is forced to face
its unimportance, that gives each individual the right to
take revenge by making himself master over his own
imaginary universe. If you're thinking of becoming a
misanthrope and want to know if I think it's a good idea
why don't you just ask me instead of trying to make me
feel sorry for you

MR SMITH: Jesus. I'm going to eat, I'm hungry

BUBBLES: Shall I come?

MR SMITH: No, you've just had your breakfast

*   *   *

MR GREENHOUSE: There's something I'd like to show
you. Have you got a minute. Mr Smith?

MR SMITH: Ok Mr Greenhouse

MR GREENHOUSE: Here, look out there in the garden

MR SMITH: What is it?

MR GREENHOUSE: Can't you see? The plaster is coming
off the wall

MR SMITH: Oh. Well?

MR GREENHOUSE: Damp, you see. I was wondering,
would you fix it for me?

MR SMITH: Me?

MR GREENHOUSE: Yes, just a bit of plastering. One needs the walls to be in good working order, don't you think?

MR SMITH: I couldn't do it all

MR GREENHOUSE: No, just the bit where it's coming away

MR SMITH: Alright. I come from a family of plasterers actually

MR GREENHOUSE: That's what I thought

*   *   *

BUBBLES: Where are you going with that?

MR SMITH: I'm just going to fix a bit of the wall in the garden

BUBBLES: But what about our party? Won't you waltz with me?

MR SMITH: I like to be useful

BUBBLES: That strikes me as a bit peculiar

MR SMITH: A garden wall never did anyone any harm. Or are you so young you confuse a garden wall with the walls of a prison?

BUBBLES: What an incredible outburst. Go and mend the wall if you want to

MR SMITH: I don't understand, you used to be a nice sensible girl, now you're trying to make me walk and talk exactly like you

BUBBLES: No I'm not

MR SMITH: Yes, you want me to use the same words as you. You want me to be a bloody rugby player like you, you want me to sit around grimacing on my arse like you do, making lists of my opponents. Not only that, you want me to be enthusiastic about it, well let me tell you, if I thought as you do I'd give it up, I'd give up thinking altogether. I'd rather lay on my back bleating. I'd rather die. I'd rather give up my soul.

BUBBLES: You just did.

MR SMITH: Yes I just did.

*   *   *

In the hall, party in the other room.

MARVIN: You still here then, why is that?

MR SMITH: I'd rather not say Marvin

MARVIN: You don't have to, my sister has told me all about it

MR SMITH: She did?

MARVIN: Yes, actually there's something I'd like to ask you if you don't mind

MR SMITH: Yes?

MARVIN: Bubbles said you are perverse, You distort the obvious into the unrecognizable

MR SMITH: She said that?

MARVIN: "Sometimes" she said "I think to myself, what am I doing here with this man who deliberately misunderstands half of what I say and who turns my actions on their heads, so that I am transformed into a grotesque monster, a narrow-minded country bumpkin and a bourgeois doctrinaire with no love no subtlety and no sense of humour."

MR SMITH: Well I –

MARVIN: "Doesn't he think I feel lonely enough without him betraying me in this way"

MR SMITH: I –

MARVIN: "He needs to find the enemy in a place he can really hurt it, in the poor heart of one who loves him and whom he loves"

MR SMITH: Yes, I see. Well that's all very true. May I ask what you do all day?

MARVIN: I study! I'm going mad with study. I study and study and study. I'm obsessed if you like. Call me a fool but in actual fact I care about what I'm doing. Perhaps you think that's funny? Or a bit queer. But someone's got to care about something. I believe in the future

MR SMITH: That's very good to hear. What... drives you on?

MARVIN: A love of humanity

MR SMITH: I'm amazed

MARVIN: Don't be amazed. It's probably just because your greater knowledge and experience acts as a depressant upon your imagination

MR SMITH: You are an extraordinary young man. Would you forgive me if I go and lie down?

MARVIN: Aren't you going back in to join the Hawaiian dancing?

MR SMITH: I'm not quite sure what's expected of me

MARVIN: Don't worry, they've seen the worn out depressed state you're in. I don't think they're expecting miracles

*   *   *

Inside the party.

MRS FISCHBEIN: You can call me Mrs Fischbein. Would you like to buy one of my paintings?

MR SMITH: Mrs Fischbein, if that really is your name, you should take it easy. You'll wear yourself out at that rate

MRS FISCHBEIN: Do I look worn? Is that what you mean?

MR SMITH: You are out of control Mrs Fischbein. You talk rubbish

MRS FISCHBEIN: And you're right. You've seen right through me

MR SMITH: But not. Is that what you mean?

MRS FISCHBEIN: Of course I mean that! What kind of a dog do you think I am? Do you take me for a fool Mr... Mr what?

MR SMITH: Mr Smith

MRS FISCHBEIN: What are you doing here? What are you doing at this party? I don't recognise you. Are you new on the scene? Yes I see it now, it's your eyes, your wonderful blue eyes. Would you like to come for a walk?

MR SMITH: I have to serve the drinks

MRS FISCHBEIN: Fuck. You're not a butler?

MR SMITH: I'm a personal friend

MRS FISCHBEIN: You'd better not be a hanger-on. I love these people. They are my family. Get me a drink

MR SMITH: I'm really sorry but the wine has run out

MRS FISCHBEIN: But it's only 9.30. You're joking!

MR SMITH: No, really

MRS FISCHBEIN: You'd better get me some wine or someone will get hurt. I can be violent

MR SMITH: Are you a painter then?

MRS FISCHBEIN: Try and guess

MR SMITH: Alright; No, you're not.

MRS FISCHBEIN: Wrong. I am. I love my work. I live for it. I would die for it. In a hail of bullets I would step forward.

MR SMITH: I don't think anyone would bother to fire bullets at a painter

MRS FISCHBEIN: They would, because I'm young, I'm fearless

MR SMITH: Nonsense

MRS FISCHBEIN: You could be right. But you know it's not about that. You're not stupid, you're clever. Very clever. Very, very clever. In fact you are an artist. You are a painter. You are a better painter than me. Don't deny it because that would be a bore, a downright bore!

MR SMITH: You are a bore Mrs Fischbein

MRS FISCHBEIN: That's because I haven't got a drink. Get me one or I'll cut that girl over there's arm with this penknife

MR SMITH: That's ridiculous

MRS FISCHBEIN: Ask around. They'll tell you I'm capable of it, you'd better do something

MR SMITH: All there is now is water

MRS FISCHBEIN: Is everyone else drinking water?

MR SMITH: A glass of water is good for the kidneys

MR GREENHOUSE: Mr Smith. There you are. I'm sorry to have caused you all this embarrassment. Do we have any bottles hidden away? I forgot to ask

MR SMITH: How would I know Mr Greenhouse?

MR GREENHOUSE: Well we don't. I can tell you that actually. But I wanted to check with you

MRS FISCHBEIN: You sod! Asking me here to drink water!

MR GREENHOUSE: Look Mrs Fischbein, this is a celebration, not just of corporal things but of spiritual things, it's what you could call an engagement party, a uniting of sundered entities, a spiritual revival

MRS FISCHBEIN: But who are you talking about?

MR GREENHOUSE: Mr Smith. Mr Smith has promised to marry my daughter

MRS FISCHBEIN: That's nice of him

MR GREENHOUSE: Yes it is

MRS FISCHBEIN: Why have you got him serving the... water

MR GREENHOUSE: Because I wanted to. Do you mind?

MRS FISCHBEIN: Does he mind?

MR GREENHOUSE: He doesn't mind. He likes it

MRS FISCHBEIN: You empty minded sod. I'm going to attack someone

MR GREENHOUSE: Violence violence everywhere. You bitch, you vicious bitch! It's people like you –

MRS FISCHBEIN: Yes, go on. You were going to say?

MR GREENHOUSE: It doesn't matter. My thoughts are all confused. I'm too upset. I hate violence

MRS FISCHBEIN: Then why did you stab, me?

MR GREENHOUSE: I didn't!

MRS FISCHBEIN: You did

MR GREENHOUSE: That was years ago. I was a young man

MRS FISCHBEIN: You were a pimp. He stabbed me in my ear, Mr Smith, and I had to be taken to hospital in a taxi. I was the laughing stock

MR GREENHOUSE: They all loved you though didn't they? The doctors even tried to seduce you in your hospital bed

MRS FISCHBEIN: Here take my knife. Stab me again. See what happens

MR GREENHOUSE: I wouldn't waste my time. Nothing would happen. Just more conversation, more telephone calls. More money being spent needlessly, more, more, more. More of the same

MRS FISCHBEIN: You think bandages are a waste of time. That Spanish family with their twisted ankles, were they a waste of time?

MR GREENHOUSE: Of course not. They were decent people. I'm not a complete madman

MRS FISCHBEIN: Let me tell you what your problem is. You've got nothing left to live for, you don't believe in anything anymore, you don't love anyone, you've no real thoughts in your head even

MR GREENHOUSE: I have got bloody thoughts! You bitch. I'm thinking from dawn to dusk. I think in my fucking sleep. Look at the world for God's sake, the

rotten stinking mess. Who wouldn't think. Everyone
thinks. They think about the love that's been lost,
the lives that have been mercilessly, callously thrown
away, like fish, that's right, I said fish. Ah yes, now
you remember don't you, the way you used to enjoy
slaughtering fish

MRS FISCHBEIN: It was my job to kill fish

MR GREENHOUSE: And how you enjoyed it!

MRS FISCHBEIN: So that is what you live for, these
maudlin thoughts

MR GREENHOUSE: I live for joy, yes joy. The joy of life

MRS FISCHBEIN: The joy of life?

MR GREENHOUSE: That's right

MRS FISCHBEIN: And where is it?

MR GREENHOUSE: Where is it?

MRS FISCHBEIN: Yes, where is it?

MR GREENHOUSE: It's here. In my house

MRS FISCHBEIN: In this little house, there is joy?
Do you think so? Have you asked your children?
Have you asked your ex-wife? This man, Mr Smith,
your son-in-law to be, have you asked him at all?

MR GREENHOUSE: I've asked. I haven't got around to
Mr Smith yet, but I will eventually

MRS FISCHBEIN: What did they say?

MR GREENHOUSE: Do you want to know? They said
Daddy, life is a damn sight better now after you've got
rid of that Mrs Fischbein because when one went to the
toilet after her there was a stench of chemicals from the
drugs in her blood. It made us all feel sick

MRS FISCHBEIN: You've embarrassed Mr Smith.
Do you like all this shit-talk Mr Smith. Does it interest
you at all?

MR SMITH: Not really

MRS FISCHBEIN: You see

MR GREENHOUSE: I'm sorry Mr Smith, it seems I've
gone too far and caused you embarrassment. When I first
met Mrs Fischbein she was miraculous. We don't know
when to stop anymore

MRS FISCHBEIN: I've only just started.

She grabs a young girl aged twenty and puts her in a headlock.

Now let's see. This little bitch gets her arms stabbed
unless I get some red wine

LITTLE NEIGHBOUR GIRL: Let go of me

MRS FISCHBEIN: (*Slaps her.*) Be quiet

MR GREENHOUSE: We've got a crisis on our hands

MRS FISCHBEIN: Why don't you just stop behaving like
a prick and get me what I want

LITTLE NEIGHBOUR GIRL: Ow!

MRS FISCHBEIN: Does that hurt lovey? Where are you
from?

LITTLE NEIGHBOUR GIRL: Piss off. I'm a neighbour

MRS FISCHBEIN: Why are you here? Is it for the
drinkies or are you hoping one of the men here might
put his hand up your dress, like this?

*The LITTLE NEIGHBOUR GIRL makes a silent grimace, a slight
moan of neither pain nor pleasure.*

She's stopped talking, she likes it

LITTLE NEIGHBOUR GIRL: No I don't

MR SMITH: Well that's lucky

MR GREENHOUSE: What's lucky Mr Smith?

MR SMITH: It seems there's some wine here

MR GREENHOUSE: No that's water I'm afraid

MR SMITH: No it's wine, look!

MR GREENHOUSE: I don't believe it. That's astonishing!
I poured water into that jug only ten minutes ago

MR SMITH: Well it's wine now

MR GREENHOUSE: Listen everybody. There's been a
miracle. Listen! There's been a miracle performed here
tonight. Mr Smith here has turned this jug of water into
wine. So... gather round with your glasses, one at a time
please

*　　*　　*

Train tracks.

MRS FISCHBEIN: Please Mr Smith, walk along these
train tracks with me. It's the short cut to my house.
It will only take a few minutes. You're not afraid of
trains are you?

MR SMITH: It depends

MRS FISCHBEIN: I promise you we'll jump out of the
way if one comes. Come on

They walk.

There's something I've been meaning to ask you all
night Mr Smith, I think you know what it is?

MR SMITH: No, I don't

MRS FISCHBEIN: I want you to meet me in a secret place.

MR SMITH: I couldn't, I'm engaged to marry

MRS FISCHBEIN: To marry whom?

MR SMITH: You know, Mr Greenhouse's daughter, Bubbles

MRS FISCHBEIN: You grit your jaw when you say her name. Why's that? Aren't you in love with her?

MR SMITH: Yes. Yes I am

MRS FISCHBEIN: It's odd you see because she strikes me as being not really your type, she seems... too tall for you

MR SMITH: That can't be helped I'm afraid

MRS FISCHBEIN: Too large all in all. Too large a personality. I imagine you'd prefer the quiet mousy type, someone a bit more like me. Would you hold my arm, my shoes are getting caught on the sleepers. So, you're willing to take her as she is?

MR SMITH: (*Laughs a little laugh.*) Yes, that's right

MRS FISCHBEIN: That's not very romantic

MR SMITH: Yes it is. It's extremely romantic, to be willing to overlook...

MRS FISCHBEIN: Yes?

MR SMITH: Someone's faults. To forgive them. That's love

MRS FISCHBEIN: It sounds like contempt to me

MR SMITH: What would you know about it

MRS FISCHBEIN: You're right. And I don't wish to know either. I don't want to be tolerated I want to be adored. I want someone who will never let me out of their sight, who will follow me across the room with their eyes. And

that is a way of being free Mr Smith. You're not listening
to me at all. What are you thinking about? It's Bubbles
isn't it?

MR SMITH: I'm not in the mood for conversation,
Mrs Fischbein

MRS FISCHBEIN: Yes I know, it's all inner life with
you isn't it. I can see it in your lovely eyes. But on the
outside – nothing. Empty, worthless, mean and selfish.
I know, as soon as I'm gone you'll be walking back
alone, as gay as a little bird thinking and laughing to
yourself. Whereas I will be alone and sad, not gay at all.
Isn't that funny?

MR SMITH: Mrs Fischbein

MRS FISCHBEIN: Would you mind if I wrote to you?
May I?

MR SMITH: If you want to

MRS FISCHBEIN: You see! I'm becoming more appealing
to you now. You can pity me

MR SMITH: Not at all

MRS FISCHBEIN: But you wouldn't like to be me

MR SMITH: No I wouldn't like to be you

MRS FISCHBEIN: I bet you have lots of women writing
to you

MR SMITH: No, none

MRS FISCHBEIN: Liar. Still you don't have to write back
but you must read them, no matter what I say in them.
Do you promise?

MR SMITH: Yes alright

MRS FISCHBEIN: Am I boring you?

MR SMITH: I am in love Mrs Fischbein, I'm sorry

MRS FISCHBEIN: Never mind. It must be painful for you to be here with me. You can go now, I'll walk on alone. Look out a train!

A train approaches, but it stops. Someone gets out of the train and walks down the tracks towards them. They stand in the train's lights. It is hissing and rumbling like a beast.

MR BARON: Freddy, Freddy, Fred Smith! It *is* you!

MR SMITH: It's my boss

MR BARON: I thought it was you. I was smoking a cigar out of the window and I saw you so I pulled the chord. You madman, what are you doing here?

MR SMITH: We're taking a short cut. This is Mrs Fischbein, this is Mr Baron

MR BARON: Pleased to meet you. Why haven't you been in to work? Are you ill?

MR SMITH: I'm sorry I should have called in

MR BARON: If you're unwell you should be at home wrapped up warm

MR SMITH: Should we try to move out of the way?

MR BARON: Yes. Let's go through this fence. Do you mind Mrs Fishwife?

MRS FISCHBEIN: No, I'd be happy to join you. I live just here anyway

MR BARON: Actually I love climbing over fences. It gives me a sense of rebellion, freedom. Like when one was a child and habitually played where one wasn't allowed. Mind the barbs

MRS FISCHBEIN: Look I've picked these blackberries. Would you like one Mr Baron?

MR BARON: How delicious

MR SMITH: How's Mrs Baron?

MR BARON: We shouldn't complain Mrs Baron and I. Life has its pleasures. Don't you think so Mrs Fishwife?

MRS FISCHBEIN: Yes I agree with you

MR BARON: Are you married?

MRS FISCHBEIN: Yes I am. This is my house actually. Oh look there's my husband in the doorway

MR BARON: What does your husband do for a living?

MRS FISCHBEIN: He's a diplomat

From the doorway some way off, Mr Fischbein.

MR FISCHBEIN: There you are you bitch! Get in here quick, wait till I get my hands on you. Who are those fucking pimps with you? Clear off before I come and smash your faces in

MRS FISCHBEIN: I'll say goodnight then

MR BARON: Yes, goodnight Mrs Fischbein

MR SMITH: Yes, goodnight

MR BARON: I think we'd better make ourselves scarce don't you Mr Smith?

MRS FISCHBEIN: *(Calls to MR SMITH from the doorway.)* Goodnight darling!

She is seized roughly. We hear the sound of heavy slaps, screaming and crying.

MR BARON: Do you think you'll be in to work in the next few days?

MR SMITH: To be honest I don't know. I'm in the grips of something undefinable

MR BARON: Don't despair. You're still young. The world is at your feet

MR SMITH: I don't want it there, ugly thing. It's going from bad to worse

MR BARON: Yes, I see, where's the comfort in that

MR SMITH: That one will soon be dead

MR BARON: Not all that soon necessarily

MR SMITH: I ask myself; What shall I do for the next forty years?

MR BARON: Doesn't this apparent loss of idealism simply mean that although you can't change the world in the way you thought you could change it, you must then turn and begin with yourself. For it is by changing yourself that you change the world

MR SMITH: Ah, the transcendental approach. I am afraid my thinking rarely soars to such heights

MR BARON: Remember how as a child one always saw the great potential in everything

MR SMITH: The great potential, yes

MR BARON: Now everywhere you look there is cruelty and slaughter, mindlessness and stupidity, and bad manners. Sometimes I hate life and I want to die. It frightens me to be alive in this world

MR SMITH: Yes

MR BARON: Shall I arrange a couple of weeks off work?

*   *   *

Sounds of a scuffle, glasses and insults are thrown, furniture is knocked over, blows are struck. MR SMITH returns to the house and is greeted by MR GREENHOUSE who is pulling one end of a stretcher, upon which reclines MRS BULIMA.

MR GREENHOUSE: Help me with this stretcher please. Rest there now Mrs Bulima

MR SMITH: What on earth has happened?

MR GREENHOUSE: It's terrible Mr Smith, terrible

MR SMITH: The party ended in a fight did it?

MR GREENHOUSE: What? Oh this mess you mean. Yes there was a small fight, a squabble. But that's nothing. No, something dreadful has happened

MR SMITH: What?

MR GREENHOUSE: That little neighbour girl has done something unspeakable upstairs

MR SMITH: Really? What did she do?

MR GREENHOUSE: I couldn't possibly speak it. But it was hideous. Mrs Bulima here nearly passed away when she saw it. Who would have thought that innocent looking girl would have such violence inside her. It's sick, sick!

MR SMITH: Where is the little neighbour girl now?

MR GREENHOUSE: I don't know but when I see her I'll give her a piece of my mind. Not that I blame her, no. Her parents must have done something unspeakable to her. I've a good mind to go round and ask them. Sick! Sick! Sick! How are you feeling now Mrs Bulima

MRS BULIMA: I'm perfectly alright Mr Greenhouse, I don't know what all the fuss is about

MR GREENHOUSE: Your pulse disappeared entirely for a few moments that's what. We were worried you might also be brain dead

MRS BULIMA: Well, well, I'm not anyway. I'd like a vol-au-vent

MR GREENHOUSE: I'm dreadfully sorry for what happened

MRS BULIMA: Nonsense. One gets used to this sort of thing. This is the kind of society we live in now. I read a book about it. It's called the democratisation of outrage. You see why should governments have a monopoly on unspeakable cruelty and outrage? It's inevitable that in the wake of the first world war and the gas camps and in the shadow of the bomb that the ordinary people fight back with horrors of their own.

MR GREENHOUSE: That's all very well Mrs Bulima but where does it lead?

MRS BULIMA: To greater... more... freedom. I think.

MR GREENHOUSE: I see. Well that girl was a wolf in sheep's clothing. I don't think she's interested in anyone's freedom but her own

MRS BULIMA: That is her democratic right don't you think so Mr Greenhouse

MR GREENHOUSE: But does it make anything better?

MRS BULIMA: Oh it's all such a muddle

MR GREENHOUSE: Ah, there she is. Now listen to me young lady, I want a word with you

LITTLE NEIGHBOUR GIRL: Oh piss off

MR GREENHOUSE: Now you stop right there

LITTLE NEIGHBOUR GIRL: Get your hands off me you old molester

MR GREENHOUSE: How dare you! You ignorant little bitch!

LITTLE NEIGHBOUR GIRL: Rape! Help! Rape!

FRIEND: What's the matter Tricksie?

LITTLE NEIGHBOUR GIRL: This cunt

FRIEND: Get your filthy hands off her you old git or you'll get a smack in the mouth. Come on Trix...

They move off.

MR GREENHOUSE: Well how do you like that!

MRS BULIMA: They have very little respect it's true

MR GREENHOUSE: They lose respect for the older generation before earning any respect for themselves

MRS BULIMA: They watch too much television

MR GREENHOUSE: And the schools and their parents are too soft on them

MRS BULIMA: And of course there's no work for them to do

MR SMITH: What did she do, the little neighbour girl?

MR GREENHOUSE: She killed three people

MR SMITH: What?

MR GREENHOUSE: Yes, it was carnage up there. Unfortunately she chopped up the bodies into such tiny pieces there's really no proof. We had a head count but some people had already gone home so we don't know who's missing until the morning

MR SMITH: But are you sure?

MR GREENHOUSE: Oh yes, she showed it all to us before she flushed it away

MR SMITH: But I'm speechless. And you just let her go?

MRS BULIMA: Mr Greenhouse did try dear

MR GREENHOUSE: No, he's right. I think whipping's too good for them

MRS BULIMA: It does very little good I'm afraid that sort of thing

MR GREENHOUSE: Or a good long prison sentence of course

MRS BULIMA: You're probably right I suppose, who knows?

MR GREENHOUSE: They should definitely be punished

MRS BULIMA: You're right Mr Greenhouse I'm sure. Could I have that vol-au-vent now please, my appetite is reviving. Perhaps you could carry me in to the running buffet

He doesn't, she walks indoors.

MR SMITH: I don't know what to say. Where's Bubbles?

MR GREENHOUSE: Ah yes, well she's gone. She asked me to give you this (*A letter.*)

MR SMITH: I see

MR GREENHOUSE: What does it say?

MR SMITH: She says she's gone away, she couldn't bear it anymore. Couldn't bear what I wonder?

MR GREENHOUSE: Do you need to ask? Are you so heartless that you can't see you've broken her heart?

MR SMITH: Oh yes and how did I do that?

MR GREENHOUSE: How? How? In all sorts of ways

MR SMITH: What ways?

MR GREENHOUSE: All sorts

MR SMITH: I see. And what about you? You must be the worst sort of father

MR GREENHOUSE: Oh yes? In what way?

MR SMITH: In what way? I'll tell you in what way!

MR GREENHOUSE: Go on tell me

MR SMITH: She's told me you forget her name

MR GREENHOUSE: Rubbish I never forget her name. You on the other hand seem to forget her completely. Apparently, apparently you don't even like her

MR SMITH: I do like her

MR GREENHOUSE: Not very much apparently

MR SMITH: That's hardly my fault. She's not very nice

MR GREENHOUSE: My daughter, not very nice?

MR SMITH: That's right, You know it. I know. So let's stop beating around the bush

MR GREENHOUSE: Alright what's wrong with her?

MR SMITH: Firstly, she's ugly. Secondly, I can't remember, thirdly she's bossy and fourthly she's too tall and she smells. She behaves as if she's fifty when in fact she's only twenty-six. When I ask her for something she looks at me as if I'm a schoolboy and says "Do you think you deserve it?" And she's false. When she smiles it's false. I'd rather she didn't smile at all. I don't need smiles all the time especially if they're false

MR GREENHOUSE: So, I'll tell her not to smile

MR SMITH: Don't tell her not to smile! Don't tell her not to smile. She isn't smiling. She must know she isn't smiling. Unless she's stupid as well. You can't tell her don't smile because she won't know what you're talking about

MR GREENHOUSE: All I can say is she seems to be getting on your nerves

MR SMITH: Getting on my nerves? She's not getting on my nerves! She just doesn't know her bloody job. For all her busyness she's completely ineffective at her own bloody job

MR GREENHOUSE: What do you mean 'her job'?

MR SMITH: How should I know? How could anybody know. She's so completely ineffectual there's no guessing what her bloody job is. You know what?; it's anybody's guess what she's supposed to be doing. Anybody's guess

MR GREENHOUSE: I see

MR SMITH: I mean I wouldn't mind her being such a frump, such a supercilious, sneering, overbearing lump if she at least were pulling her weight. But she isn't. She leaves it all undone. She lets everybody else do everything and then, when she does do something, she does it at the wrong time, in the wrong place, in the wrong way. And what's worse is, when finally at the last minute she does hand you the – whatever it is – half broken fucked up, ruined... er... object, whatever it is, she gives you this funny kind of look, which, I don't know if it's meant to be a superior kind of look or what it is, but there's one thing clear and that is – she thinks she's done you a favour

MR GREENHOUSE: Well if you're not getting on...

MR SMITH: Getting on? You can either get on with her or not get on with her but in fact it doesn't make any difference. I get on with her, I get on with her, but that doesn't alter the fact that there's nothing to get on with. She's empty. She's just – well what is she? She's a body and a collection of facial expressions. She can frown, yes she can do that albeit involuntarily, and she can broaden her mouth into that smile thing, and she can do something with one of her eyes, I don't know if maybe it's a glass eye – is it a glass eye? – or if it's a twinkle she's got there in one of her eyes, perhaps it is, alright, but if it is I wouldn't like to know what's behind it

MR GREENHOUSE: This comes as a great surprise to me. I've always been led to believe that she, what is it her mother said about her? She's "full of emotion", yes that's it, she's full of emotion

MR SMITH: Alright Mr Greenhouse. I can see now that you know next to nothing about your daughter and that I'm talking to the wrong person

MR GREENHOUSE: Well I wouldn't say that but it's true I'm not the world's authority on her

MR SMITH: Well who is, just as a matter of interest?

MR GREENHOUSE: Her mother knows her awfully well, awfully well, but she lives in Barcelona. I had a girlfriend once, they seemed to get along alright, they were closer in age you see, but she left to become a tour guide

MR SMITH: Mr Greenhouse, why is it you don't protect your innocent daughter against attack?

MR GREENHOUSE: I see, well no-one is quite innocent Mr Smith. And it was quite some attack

MR SMITH: It was unfounded Mr Greenhouse

MR GREENHOUSE: Well I don't know then Mr Smith

MR SMITH: How could she survive such a deluge of wrongs?

MR GREENHOUSE: By learning to swim I expect Mr Smith

MR SMITH: What time is it?

MR GREENHOUSE: It's three in the morning

MR SMITH: I'm tired now, Mr Greenhouse, I'm tired.
I'd like to sleep here on the floor if you don't mind

*   *   *

Next morning, dawn (3 hours later). MR SMITH asleep on the ground.
MR GREENHOUSE comes in.

MR GREENHOUSE: Good morning Mr Smith! Rise and
shine!

MR SMITH: What time is it?

MR GREENHOUSE: Six thirty. I've been thinking about
you Mr Smith, all morning

MR SMITH: *All* morning?

MR GREENHOUSE: What kind of life have you
had? You seem a sensible mature sort of a chap, so
I wondered

MR SMITH: I've had a great life Mr Greenhouse.
I've received nothing but praise

MR GREENHOUSE: You've a helpful, tolerant kind of
attitude most of the time haven't you? You seem a mild,
moderate sort

MR SMITH: I try to be mild and moderate. People
like that

MR GREENHOUSE: They do don't they. I'm not mild or
moderate. I'm a tiger, and I don't give a damn. I've come
this far and I won't give an inch do you understand me?
You know what life is like, you know what it's about.
First you hope you can change the world for the better
then you realise you can't, then you set up alarms on
your windows and keep a shotgun by the backdoor.
That's it isn't it?

MR SMITH: That's it Mr Greenhouse

MR GREENHOUSE: I won't give a fucking inch. I used to weep when I watched the news, still do. But when you've got no religion and no political beliefs you're on your own staring at the wall wondering whether to cut your wrists. After that it just depends whether you've got a cheerful nature or not. I haven't got a particularly cheerful nature Mr Smith, not really

MR SMITH: Is there any breakfast?

MR GREENHOUSE: Bubbles said to give you this

MR SMITH: What is it?

MR GREENHOUSE: A sandwich

MR SMITH: For breakfast? What do you mean 'Bubbles'

MR GREENHOUSE: She came back. Picked up all the broken glass then went off again

MR SMITH: The sandwich is ice cold

MR GREENHOUSE: What keeps me alive Mr Smith is my inner life. It's not king or country, I don't even like this bloody country, and it's not a belief in folklore or psychology or anything else. I'm not a fucking art collector Mr Smith. You see all those books in there? I've read every one of them, and I can't remember a single word. Would that irritate you Mr Smith, if you read a thousand or so books from around the world, of philosophy and literature and didn't find it left any significant residue? Well I don't find it annoys me at all because it's just a pastime. What the hell else would it be anyway for God's sake?

MR SMITH: Would you give me some money, I'd like to go away on a little holiday

MR GREENHOUSE: Would you?

MR SMITH: Yes I'd like to get away from it all but I'm in debt. A day or two away would cheer me up

MR GREENHOUSE: But how do we know you'd come back? How do we know you wouldn't just run off with some girlie or other and not look back

MR SMITH: Because sadly I can't ignore my responsibilities

MR GREENHOUSE: Everyone has their responsibilities. Even if you were a wild savage you'd have those. Or even a wild beast. Or a gypsy or a fly or an antelope. Don't be ashamed of a generous nature

MR SMITH: So, fifty quid?

MR GREENHOUSE: I don't have it. Never have any money, I don't know why. Is it my age? I don't know. Am I not perhaps useful anymore? Society rewards those most useful to it doesn't it? Rubbish. Money rewards money! Nobody gives a damn Mr Smith

MR SMITH: No

MR GREENHOUSE: Do you know what I read the other day? That if I say something absurd it will make you want to disagree with it

MR SMITH: Go on then

MR GREENHOUSE: Alright – Actually I can't think of anything absurd to say. Nothing seems absurd enough to require disagreement. My cooked breakfast calls me Mr Smith. (*MRS BULIMA comes out again.*) Ah Mrs Bulima, I expect you are responsible for those sizzling rashers, let's waste no more time (*Goes.*)

MRS BULIMA: A certain someone asked me to give you this Mr Smith. It is a letter, as you can see. Your secret is safe with me. I have known illicit love. I have known it

within these walls. I even think there was a moment
last night when you opened a door and caught sight –
tactfully you turned away and put it out of your mind.
I – we are so grateful

MR SMITH: Think nothing of it

MRS BULIMA: And I wish you good luck. I think the
young should prosper in all that they do

MR SMITH: Thankfully they don't

*   *   *

A small airport.

MR SMITH: When is take off?

MR GREENHOUSE: Ten to three

MR SMITH: How long is the flight?

MR GREENHOUSE: Ten minutes

MR SMITH: Good

MR GREENHOUSE: We fly towards the darkened sun for
a few minutes and it's all over

MR SMITH: It's such a relief

MR GREENHOUSE: Why, if you don't mind me asking,
why are you taking this flight. Everyone knows you hate
the thought of Australasia

MR SMITH: I had no choice. You see... I've lost my sense
of humour

MR GREENHOUSE: Oh no. Whatever caused that?

MR SMITH: Certainly nothing I shouldn't have been
able to deal with perfectly easily. My temperament
though, works against my true nature. And so I must
pay the price

MR GREENHOUSE: That really is jolly bad luck

MR SMITH: It smells like a farmyard in here. It smells like a pigsty, why is that?

MR GREENHOUSE: Did I tell you you've been invited to the captain's cabin?

MR SMITH: I am terrified of heights you know. But still, I'm looking forward to seeing the archipelago beneath me. All the tiny little islands. It's not far is it?

MR GREENHOUSE: It's a short hop. Ten minutes

MR SMITH: I shall accept it. I shall think that it's me flying as if I were a bird

MR GREENHOUSE: Ah, here's the captain

MR SMITH: Bubbles, is it you?

BUBBLES: Hello

MR SMITH: You look bigger and stronger than ever in your uniform. So you're at the controls?

BUBBLES: That's right. You don't mind?

MR SMITH: Of course not. Do you have time for me to ask you a few questions Bubbles? When's my birthday? What's my favourite animal? Plain chocolate or milk chocolate? Venice or Florence? Fleas or lice?

BUBBLES: Lice

MR SMITH: Correct. There's no fooling you is there

BUBBLES: I have to go now. See you in a few minutes

MR GREENHOUSE: I hate these travelling types. Adventure, adventure, adventure. Why can't she stay at home. What's so different about somewhere else? She's still the same godawful fucking person anyway isn't she, when she gets back

MR SMITH: I must say I like the look of her in that uniform though, I'm sure I'll be safe in her hands

MR GREENHOUSE: In the old days, let's say in Napoleon's time, you could lay down with your depression, put your head upon a stone and watch the water trickle in the field and look up at the sky. You could say "I am a wretch, Mankind is wretched, But the skies... are great and endless." Now man has pulled down the sky and the universe and invented its destruction. Now there is nowhere to lay your head with your depression for you must say "The universe is a wretched thing, Mankind can turn it into a lamb chop"

MR SMITH: A lamb chop?

MR GREENHOUSE: Yes, haven't you heard? A machine to make this into that ad infinitum. It's free frigidaires for all

MR SMITH: I'm a bit worried about the time. I think I should go on board. Goodbye then

MR GREENHOUSE: Oh no, I'm coming with you, didn't I say? Mrs Fischbein and I are reviving our old love affair and running away together. She's already installed in the best seats by the window

MR SMITH: I see. Alright then

MR GREENHOUSE: Yes, alright. I suppose it is alright? You don't feel as if you are the one who ought to be having this rendez-vous with Mrs Fischbein?

MR SMITH: Of course not. The fat bitch. I hate her!

MR GREENHOUSE: Touchy

MR SMITH: Yes I'm touchy, I'm sick of it, I'm sick of all of you. Get out of my way

*   *   *

In flight.

MRS FISCHBEIN: xbxbdh hdjdk

MR SMITH: I can't hear you Mrs Fischbein!

MRS FISCHBEIN: dkbmghfyeiei

MR SMITH: No, it's no good. The engine noise!

MRS FISCHBEIN: Come And Sit Next To Me!

MR SMITH: (*Does so.*) Alright

MRS FISCHBEIN: Drink? Cig? Shall I order you a meal?

MR SMITH: No!

MRS FISCHBEIN: What?

MR SMITH: No! Too nervous

MRS FISCHBEIN: Why?

MR SMITH: Doesn't matter! Where is Mr Greenhouse?

MRS FISCHBEIN: How should I know? Isn't the view
     fantastic!

     MR SMITH looks, sits back down.

     thgdbshshchxxxsx

MR SMITH: Can't hear

MRS FISCHBEIN: fkcksxkfincuxstfk

MR SMITH: Can't hear

MRS FISCHBEIN: (*Tries to kiss him.*) Please suck my
     breasts!

MR SMITH: What are you doing?

MRS FISCHBEIN: I love you! I want you! You are like
     Napoleon! I was your Egypt, now you are flying to
     St Helens. Oh my chronicler! Reveal me to the world!

MR SMITH: (*Disengaging himself.*) Alright Mrs Fischbein, I will. But first I have an important engagement... in the captain's cabin

He staggers up the gangway as the plane lurches about. MR GREENHOUSE bursts out of the cabin. Cabin door opens, radio noises, electronics. Closes.

MR GREENHOUSE: Don't go in there boy! Don't go in! She can't do it. She can't fly this thing. I'm sorry to admit it but it's true

MR SMITH: It's what?

MR GREENHOUSE: It's true!

MR SMITH: (*Can't hear, shrugs.*)

MR GREENHOUSE: Oh out of my way! Stretcher!

MR SMITH: Bubbles, Bubbles, open the door!

BUBBLES: (*From inside the cabin.*) No! Go away!

MR SMITH: But you invited me!

BUBBLES: Please, please go away!

MR SMITH: What's going on in there?

MR GREENHOUSE rushes back with a stretcher.

MR GREENHOUSE: Out of it! Gangway! Stretcher bearer coming! (*He goes in, the door is shut in MR SMITH's face.*)

MRS FISCHBEIN: Relax darling, you look as white as a sheet. Come and join me. Did I tell you flying makes me excited? Look at the ants down there darling. Come behind me, look at them! Their little roads, their power stations! See them?

MR SMITH: I can't see a thing Mrs Fischbein

MRS FISCHBEIN: Look at the sun! Look at Phaeton's chariot, the madman, see how he's plunging through the air! Wait for me you wild man! Wait for me!

MR GREENHOUSE emerges from the cabin dragging MRS BULIMA on a stretcher.

MR GREENHOUSE: Help me with Mrs Bulima's stretcher will you Mr Smith! Calm yourself Mrs Bulima

MRS BULIMA: I don't know what all the fuss is about

MRS FISCHBEIN: Don't you Mrs Bulima, don't you? I'll tell you what it is! The day is about to end, that's all. The sun is going down!

MR GREENHOUSE: Can't you keep quiet for once

MRS BULIMA: I'm perfectly alright I tell you, I love flying

MR GREENHOUSE: I can't hear you Mrs B, speak up!

MRS BULIMA: I said, get me one of those plastic lunches

MR GREENHOUSE: Get her one of those plastic lunches will you

MRS FISCHBEIN: Let her starve. Can't you see there's no point eating now you neurotic old woman

Engines stop.

MR GREENHOUSE: What's that? The engines have stopped! Oh my God! Bubbles! Bubbles! Open up!

He goes in.

They stand in silence, the wind whistles, the plane nose-dives.

MRS FISCHBEIN: So it's too late for love now Mr Smith, I hope you're satisfied

MRS BULIMA: I don't know what all the fuss is about. This is how they fly these days. I feel perfectly alright. Of course someone should really be brought to book

MRS FISCHBEIN: What's going through your mind now Mr Smith. What's the one thought you can salvage from the wreckage to comfort you now? God is it? Or all your achievements in your field? Some little girlie? Friends, family, wife, lover?

MR GREENHOUSE: (*Returns.*) It's alright. Bubbles says she's going to glide down. It could be a bumpy landing though

BUBBLES: (*Appears.*) It's ok everyone, we're gliding down

*   *   *

On a desert island. Sand, sea, Honolulu music.

MR SMITH: That didn't seem like just ten minutes

MR GREENHOUSE: It was actually less. So, feeling glad to be on land again?

MR SMITH: It's a great relief

MR GREENHOUSE: The next flight won't be so bad

MR SMITH: What next flight? Ten minutes you said

MR GREENHOUSE: Each flight is ten minutes, but there are many of them

MR SMITH: But! How long will it be in all?

MR GREENHOUSE: Three days

MR SMITH: Three days! I can't! I can't!

MR GREENHOUSE: You're stuck I'm afraid

MR SMITH: Bubbles, Bubbles! Why didn't you tell me?

BUBBLES: What's the matter?

MR SMITH: You slug! Don't you realise what you've done? You've stranded me!

MRS FISCHBEIN: What's the matter with him?

MRS BULIMA: A little later we'll make dinner, you'll feel better

MR SMITH: Ten minutes you said, Three days!

MR GREENHOUSE: He's hysterical. Shall I get the stretcher?

MR SMITH: Yes get the stretcher. Oh no! Take me back Bubbles, please, please! I'll do anything just get me out of here. I don't feel well

BUBBLES: Darling think of the fun we'll have

MR SMITH: Don't, don't, it's not funny anymore, it's not clever anymore. It's sick! I'm serious, I can't stand it!

MRS FISCHBEIN: He's really lost his sense of humour hasn't he

MR GREENHOUSE: Listen son, you're miles from anywhere, pull yourself together

MR SMITH: You don't understand, I'm not in my right mind, I could no more pull myself together than I could stretch my wings and fly. Wait. That's an idea. I could fly back. Out of my way

MR GREENHOUSE: Quick, catch him! Don't let him near the cliff edge

He dodges about wildly trying to run off the edge of the cliff. BUBBLES stops him with a terrific blow of her mighty fist into his solar plexus.

BUBBLES: I'll get him. (*MR SMITH wheezes.*) My poor friend, did I hurt you?

MR SMITH: Bubbles you don't know your own strength

MRS BULIMA: Shall I cook something. Mr Greenhouse, you collect firewood

BUBBLES: I'm sorry everyone. No time for any of that now. Time to take off again

MRS FISCHBEIN: All this taking off and landing, it will surely drive us all mad

BUBBLES: Mrs Fischbein, I've tolerated you all my life, hanging around our house bossing me about, forgetting my birthday. But now I've had enough of you

MRS FISCHBEIN: Oh yes? I suppose you're going to punch me too in my solar plexus like you did to your poor fiancé? Just try it you overgrown urchin! I should have popped you in the oven when you were little when I had the chance

BUBBLES: Daddy, did you know Mrs Fischbein is completely bald under that wig?

MRS FISCHBEIN: Nonsense

BUBBLES: Daddy?

MR GREENHOUSE: Henrietta, it's not true is it?

MRS FISCHBEIN: Of course it isn't

BUBBLES: We'll see about that (*A brief struggle. She pulls MRS FISCHBEIN's wig off.*)

MRS FISCHBEIN: Well I told you. I'm not completely bald. I have this little tuft here, you see?

MR GREENHOUSE: Well Bubbles, she's called your bluff, she's not completely bald

BUBBLES: How can you love a woman like that? Look it's horrible!

MR GREENHOUSE: I'm surprised at you darling. I didn't know you were so narrow minded. I love Mrs Fischbein, whatever

BUBBLES: Mummy wasn't bald

MR GREENHOUSE: No, but she was a gambler and a political fanatic. I did warn her. I said; You are a bucket of bile and for that reason alone you should steer clear of politics. But did she listen? No. Now she's the poker correspondent in Las Vegas. Spending your inheritance I might add

BUBBLES: Wake up, it's time to go (*To MR SMITH.*)

MR SMITH: Again? What will become of me?

BUBBLES: New horizons darling. It's dawn. Hand me my in-flight helmet. Let's go everyone

BUBBLES pulls on her flight helmet and leads off, the rest follow unenthusiastically, except for MRS BULIMA who whistles happily.

*   *   *

PART TWO

MR SMITH and BUBBLES in an echoing country house.

Ding dong the doorbell etc.

MR GREENHOUSE comes in with MRS BULIMA and MRS FISCHBEIN.

MR GREENHOUSE: Let me look at you Bubbles.
You look lovelier than ever. So beautiful, so beautiful!
All those years! I always knew

BUBBLES: He's upstairs, he's dressing for dinner

MR GREENHOUSE: A clean shirt? Lord help us!

MRS BULIMA: This is so nice

MR GREENHOUSE: This house is a beautiful old woman;
At the head of the aged alley
The swan sang; Avenue of trees
From which the sun departs
Leave me here...

We've all missed you so much these last months. I didn't
realise how much I needed you before, your presence in
my loft, the sound of you dancing. All that, you know

MRS BULIMA: It's a romantic story darling how you came
to be here with Mr Smith. Is it still romantic? May I ask
that?

MR SMITH: (*Comes downstairs.*) Oh you've all arrived

MR GREENHOUSE: Yes, we've all arrived, did you think
some of us wouldn't make it?

MRS FISCHBEIN: We all made it Mr Smith

MR GREENHOUSE: What've you been doing with
yourself?

MR SMITH: Doing?

MRS FISCHBEIN: He's been living, Mr Greenhouse, haven't you Mr Smith?

MR SMITH: I've invited a friend, my old boss Mr Baron

MR GREENHOUSE: How old is Mr Baron?

MRS FISCHBEIN: He's younger than he looks

MR SMITH: Yes actually he's not very old. In fact he's only a few years older than me

MRS BULIMA: Don't we talk a lot about age?

MRS FISCHBEIN: Yes don't we

MRS BULIMA: Does it signify all that much do you think? You're as young as you feel. I always say that and I've always believed it

MRS FISCHBEIN: How can you believe it, it doesn't mean anything

MR SMITH: If what you say is true Mrs Bulima, I'm dead

MRS FISCHBEIN: He's dead because his heart is dead.

MR GREENHOUSE: How can you say that. Don't you see the man with his young bride? See how in love they are. Silent together while we chatter

MRS FISCHBEIN: She's got a dead man on her young hands. And when finally his body dies she will be there to put the coins on his eyes to unite at last the body to his long departed soul. But she'll be only, let me see now... fifty

MR GREENHOUSE: Nonsense

MRS FISCHBEIN: Fifty-seven. What does a woman do when she's fifty-seven?

MR GREENHOUSE: What does anyone do? I haven't
done a bloody thing for twenty years

MRS FISCHBEIN: It's a mismatch

MRS BULIMA: It may well be, but you know what
happened as well as I do

MRS FISCHBEIN: Nothing happened, a little drunkenness

MRS BULIMA: Two tee totalers

MR GREENHOUSE: Don't worry Nickette, our two lovely
hosts have gone down to the wine cellar to fetch a little
something for us

MRS BULIMA: I was telling Mrs Fischbein about love,
a story about love she likes to hear. It's about the way
these two nearly died of love for one another. I saw
it with my own eyes

MR GREENHOUSE: Is that possible?

MRS BULIMA: I was rowing them up and down the river
at Newbridge and they sat there staring at each other
until they swooned away into the water the pair of them.
I had to fish them out with the boathook

MR SMITH: Here's the wine up from the cellar but
I thought we'd go out for a walk and drink it on our feet

MR GREENHOUSE: A walk!

MR SMITH: Yes, since the sun is going down. We can walk
along the road beside the river and look for frogs in the
ditches

MRS FISCHBEIN: Frogs? What is he talking about?

MR GREENHOUSE: Coats back on everyone!

*   *   *

Outside, walking along the tarmac road beside fields and ditches, birds sing, frogs croak.

MR GREENHOUSE: So flat and calm, fields and ditches, fields and ditches. Keep up there Mrs Bulima! no skulking! Along the road here Mr Smith, is that what you had in mind? Very gay

MR SMITH: That's right Mr Greenhouse

MR GREENHOUSE: Mrs Bulima, Mrs Bulima please! You'll get lost in the undergrowth, keep out of there!

MRS BULIMA: No, Jonathan I'm not going to. I'm interested in these watermeadows. Don't you worry about me, I'm enjoying myself

MRS FISCHBEIN: Well I'm going back, it's ridiculous, it's dark

MR SMITH: No, do stay with us Mrs Fischbein, do stay with us please

MRS FISCHBEIN: (*She walks along with MR SMITH.*) I'm sorry I was so pushy with you before. So sorry. I don't know what came over me. I'd like to see how your life turns out though I admit, I was romantically attracted

MR SMITH: (*Mutters to himself.*) What on earth to?

MRS FISCHBEIN: I admit that. I can't for the life of me see what to. I mistook you for something else, I see that now and I'm sorry. Will you forgive me?

MR SMITH: Oh, of course

MRS FISCHBEIN: So does love last do you think? And do convictions become just like, you know, themes you whistle to yourself while you do the washing up? What do you think? So, do you think it's painful to fade away or just pleasant. Don't worry I won't expect you to reveal your private secret domestic life-details. I can read it in

what I call the Pain Lines. And now out of all of it you
build this beautiful thing, this house of harmony. I'll tell
you I used to resent her, The Creamy One I called her,
but I can see now that out of all of us she is the real
genius. Don't worry this isn't a curse I'm putting on
you, if it's my magic powers that worry you. It's hard
for a woman to be recognised as a genius. Unless she
produces. Do you let her produce anything? Do you?
You can tell me. Or do you have her killing spiders for
you all day long? You know, she's the sober one, she's
the one who has to try to be sexually continent. I see
the effort and the worry of it all in her lovely green eyes,
she's the guardienne of the ambition to be serious and
everlasting and eternally yours and hers and cosmically
united and all that jazz, you know

MR SMITH: Convictions Mrs Fischbein? Isn't the real
trouble remembering what they are, since one is never
required to apply them

MRS FISCHBEIN: Well, one doesn't wait to be asked Mr
Smith! Can we speak about that little disaster now, you
know we've all heard about it, and how it affected you

MR SMITH: Oh really, have you really?

MRS FISCHBEIN: Yes we read about it in the papers.
And Joanie, the little neighbour girl told us about it,
she came running in, you know how she is, all feelings
and no thoughts, or is it the other way around? She was
cursing and screaming about it all, so I said to her; Look
schmuck, people get beat up on every day, you ought to
know sweetie pie. I mean, it's like there's blood virtually
dripping from her fingers and I'm no pacifist, you know
what I mean? But didn't you rage at the way they
rounded them all up, starved them beat them and then
threw them all in the river. Have you forgotten, I mean
have you forgotten what it is to *feel* for the poor, Mr
Smith? Huh?

MR SMITH: The what?

MRS FISCHBEIN: You know, the weak, whatever. The way
their children were taken from them and sent away to
God knows where. You rogue! I bet you were on the side
of the oppressor. What a rogue you are really! You're not
even listening

MR SMITH: Excuse me Mrs Fischbein, but I think I see
my old friend Mr Baron on the horizon. I must go and
speak with him

MR BARON: (*Waving and calling in the distance.*) Yes, it's me,
it's me! (*Runs panting along the tarmac.*) Well my boy, I'm
happy to see you installed in such suitable surroundings,
a big house, lots of grand old trees around, little ditches
to play in. And she's so lovely, so lovely, so beautiful.
So exceptionally exquisite. She doesn't even need to
speak to me, I can see a certain shadow in her eye.
I know she's for you. So, your life now, has it reached
any heights at all? Are you able to be diligent at all?

MR SMITH: Diligent in what Mr Baron?

MR BARON: Oh oh, I can see nothing has changed

MR SMITH: No I'm ashamed to say it hasn't

MR BARON: Well I, Mr Smith, I have discovered the root
of a great misconception about mankind, the reason for
the failure of art, philosophy and even religion. It is this
– those who struggle in the darkness to find the hidden
lights therein are the practical end of the tool; The spirit
is in the rear end, the helpless arse

MR SMITH: I don't doubt it

MR BARON: I've given it all up, I've even given all my
money away

MR SMITH: What money?

MR BARON: I've opened a colony, I've chained myself to the railings, I've tasted the trunction Mr Smith

MR SMITH: I'm sorry to hear it

MR BARON: God feeds and clothes his sparrows but why does he neglect my children. I have millions of children Mr Smith, all over the earth

MR SMITH: We are all drops in the ocean, and the ocean gets bigger until the ocean is just a drop in another ocean and so on

MR BARON: How touching. I know it. "Futile".

MR SMITH: That's it

MR BARON: What a genius

MR GREENHOUSE and MRS FISCHBEIN come by.

MR GREENHOUSE: ... I turned on the tv the other day and saw a very peculiar thing. First a man came on and told me such and such a thing was happening, then a woman came on and told me she cared. Incredible don't you think? But which was most absurd I cannot tell

MRS FISCHBEIN: Mr Baron, your neck is ballooning out around you, have you become rich?

MR GREENHOUSE: This is stranger than fiction Mr Balloon. The sky's gone black, the crows are flying away, a big yellow cloud is billowing above us, it's as if, well it's quite as if someone is smoking a giant cigarette

MRS FISCHBEIN: To think they'd dare in this day and age

MR BARON: Isn't it just sunset?

MR GREENHOUSE: Just sunset? If it is then the sun is setting forever and forever

MR BARON: It's hard to breathe, the air is so thin

MR GREENHOUSE: It makes you wish you went training and running while there was still the chance

MRS FISCHBEIN: The sun's blotted out, it's blotted out, that's the problem

MR GREENHOUSE: It stinks around here. I think I'm having renal failure. Waste disposal

MR BARON: Relax man. There used to be a time when my sole ambition was to buy at 50 and sell at 100. Now I stay in bed most days

MR GREENHOUSE: I see. And are you happier?

MR BARON: What? No you don't understand

MRS FISCHBEIN: Mr Baboon, you really do look like an ape this evening. Your arms are even hanging

MR BARON: They are hanging a bit, I don't know why

MRS FISCHBEIN: Who's this running along the road towards us?

BUBBLES: It's my brother

MR SMITH: God, I'd almost forgotten he existed

MR GREENHOUSE: What's he running so fast for?

MR BARON: He's young, why shouldn't he run if he wants to?

MRS FISCHBEIN: But his direction is reverse, he should be running away from us towards the future, n'est-ce pas? The future we will never know, the challenge!

MR BARON: The pigswill. He's had a bellyfull of pigswill and he's running back to tell us all about it

MRS FISCHBEIN: No, no, no

MR SMITH: He's been to the shops and he's running back home to cook himself a gourmet dinner. He wants to invite us

MR GREENHOUSE: You're all wrong. He's suffering from renal failure, look at his face

MRS FISCHBEIN: What's the matter with you?

BUBBLES: Stop it, stop it all of you. He's my brother

MR BARON: He's full of shit

MRS FISCHBEIN: Mr Bacon, I'm surprised at you, you normally like everyone, you normally have a good word for everyone

MR BARON: He's an automaton, a conceited little tool, a gullible dildo for his money masters. He's a computer, a fax machine, an appointment..

MR SMITH: I always thought he was a romantic dreamy sort of chap

Marvin arrives, stops running, straightens his tie, and suit jacket, head up, straight back.

BUBBLES: Marvin darling, what's the matter?

MARVIN: What do you mean, I was jogging

BUBBLES: But you were running so fast

MARVIN: That's it sister I was running fast. But don't worry, I get here all the sooner. There's nothing to worry about

BUBBLES: Good

MARVIN: Yes, everything's ok Bubbles. I've seen God, and I've seen Satan

MR GREENHOUSE: What's wrong with you Marvin?

MR SMITH: What did God say? Marvin, tell us all

MARVIN: God wants us to say yes, but Satan, he is the negative principle, he tells us to say no

MR GREENHOUSE: No to what, in the name of Suffering Christ!

MARVIN: No, to the repast God has prepared for us. The table is set, the jugs are filled

MR GREENHOUSE: The jugs are filled with shit Marvin

MR BARON: Marvin is filled with shit

MR GREENHOUSE: I told you, renal failure

MARVIN: You blind men. Things have never been better, more... appropriate, more relevant and full of meaning

MR GREENHOUSE: That's enough Marvin, good boy

MARVIN: I've something to tell you. I've eaten Mrs Bulima

MR GREENHOUSE: What? You've eaten Mrs Bulima?

MARVIN: It was a real slap up meal I can tell you

MRS FISCHBEIN: How disgusting

MR GREENHOUSE: It's a disgrace

MR BARON: Banana anyone?

BUBBLES: Don't you hear what he said, He's eaten Mrs Bulima

MR GREENHOUSE: I'm sorry, I can't take it in. It's too much of a shock

BUBBLES: I know Daddy, you must be shocked but... your son has eaten your friend

MR GREENHOUSE: What can I say. Words fail me

MRS FISCHBEIN: Poor Mrs Bulima

BUBBLES: You! What do you care!

MRS FISCHBEIN: I care enough to say "poor
Mrs Bulima". Don't think I'm entirely without decency

MR GREENHOUSE: Marvin, You madman! I don't
believe it! Were you... hungry, or what?

MARVIN: No, no particularly hungry. Do I have to be
hungry to eat?

MR GREENHOUSE: Yes, yes actually you do. It's
indecent otherwise

MR BARON: That's right, where's your sense of decency.
Don't they teach you at that school anymore?

MARVIN: Oh yes, it's decency this decency that. Bloody
sick of it. I wanted to do Maths and R.E.

MR GREENHOUSE: Stupid boy, never listened to a word
I told him

MR BARON: Perhaps you didn't insist enough

MR GREENHOUSE: Insist? Insist on what?

MR BARON: Well, you could have imparted to him
certain... values

MR GREENHOUSE: Oh yes? Like what?

MR BARON: I don't know. Chivalry

MR GREENHOUSE: What?

MR BARON: You know, ladies first. Des Plichtes des
Gentlemen. At least it would have stopped him eating
the poor woman.

MR GREENHOUSE: (*To MARVIN.*) Would it? If I had
taught you chivalry?

MARVIN: It might have

MR GREENHOUSE: Oh... I see. Well. Perhaps I should have then

MR BARON: Something at least

MR SMITH: What happened to your utopianism Marvin?

MARVIN: Why go about dreaming of the future when the present is so fucking brilliant?

MR SMITH: Good point

MARVIN: Your trouble is, you're a misanthropist

BUBBLES: (*Quiet, almost in tears.*) Marvin, what you were saying just now, about God... I'd like to come to church with you

Pause.

MARVIN: Bubbles. It's not *that* God.

MR GREENHOUSE: My, my, everything's changing

MR BARON: Where are we exactly?

MR GREENHOUSE: I don't know. It's a bit dark to see. Mr Smith, you're our leader. Any idea?

MR SMITH: Not getting cold are we?

MR BARON: Don't tease, Mr Smith

MR GREENHOUSE: Yes come on Mr Smith, it's nearly cocoa time

MR BARON: Yes and my neck is really playing me up now

MR GREENHOUSE: Perhaps Mrs Fischbein will lend you her silky scarf

MRS FISCHBEIN: (*Reluctantly.*) Alright, alright, Let me tie it on then

She does so very tightly.

MR BARON: Steady on, you're strangling me!

MRS FISCHBEIN: I can't help it. It's this enormous thyroid!

MR BARON: I can't breathe. You're bursting my balloon!

MRS FISCHBEIN: What did you say?

MR BARON: I've swallowed my balloon. I've eaten my only means of escape. I was going to fly off with these crows (*He darts over to some crows that are hanging around nearby.*) You seven crows, come with me, I'll take you up flying in my balloon. You'll like it up there, the air is so fresh, the sky is vast, you look down and –

CROWS: We're crows, we don't need your blasted balloon. Tedious thing!

MR BARON: Damn you! If you don't accept my invitation I'll force you. I'll starve you and beat you and shout at you until you beg me to let you come

CROWS: Stand aside, live a hateful life, live a contemptible life

MR SMITH: Poor sad Mr Balloon, rejected by those he loves, chirruping away to himself. I like the man dammit. He's mad but he has a heart of gold

MR GREENHOUSE: Out of my way! (*He runs forward and seizes a crow and holds it to his head as if it is a gun.*)

MR BARON: Leave those crows alone!

MR SMITH: Whatever are you doing Mr Greenhouse? Put that crow down

MR GREENHOUSE: I'll shoot myself, I will, I will

MR SMITH: You can't shoot yourself with a bird Mr Greenhouse

MR GREEHOUSE: Oh can't I? Just watch me!

He fires a bullet from the crow but misses.

MRS FISCHBEIN: He's just shot himself with a crow

MR GREENHOUSE: Blast it! I missed!

MR SMITH: Told you

MR BARON: And you young man, look what you've driven your father to

MARVIN: Nonsense, I'm his alter ego aren't I dad? He'd love to do the things I do and say the things I say, only he's lost his nerve, ask him.

MR GREENHOUSE: It's true, I've lost my nerve, Marvin is a great inspiration. I see in him the culmination of years of.. of centuries of.. there are a few details he's overlooked of course, But he has a bright future

Pause.

Fade to...

MR BARON: I can't see a thing. Is anyone still here?

*   *   *

Birds singing, bright summer meadow sounds.

MARVIN: That's it Mr Smith, pile it high. I think my father would like his grave piled high, at least as high as your friend Mr Baron's grave and Mrs Bulima's grave. You're very good at this, I think we've found your metier. What about something to put as his headstone. A symbol of something. How about a bird?

MR SMITH: What's that a symbol of?

MARVIN: It's a symbol of flying isn't it. Don't go stupid on me Mr Smith

MR SMITH: I'm sorry

MARVIN: He looks good doesn't he Bubbles, stripped to
   the waist, all those muscles, all that sweat. Isn't he great
   Bubbles. Isn't it all so beautiful. And if it weren't for
   Daddy being dead it would be a time for a picnic or time
   to go rowing

BUBBLES: I didn't come here to go rowing. We've
   been out all night and now it's morning, I'd like to
   go home

MARVIN: But it's a beautiful day. Haven't you got a sense
   of occasion?

BUBBLES: No I haven't

MARVIN: How about you Mr Smith, have you got a sense
   of occasion?

MR SMITH: Yes I have

MARVIN: How do you get along them. I mean if you have
   got a sense of occasion and she hasn't

MR SMITH: We argue

MARVIN: No, I can't believe that. You two are so...
   innocent together

MR SMITH: Yes, well we are. We argue innocently

MARVIN: You seem afraid Mr Smith?

MR SMITH: No, I'm not afraid

MARVIN: You are

MR SMITH: Alright I am. What are you going to do
   about it?

MARVIN: But for God's sake, what are you afraid
   of? I admit it's been a shocking night, it's tragic,
   we're all sad. But what are you afraid of? Bubbles
   isn't afraid

MR SMITH: No she isn't

MARVIN: You're not afraid of *me?*

MR SMITH: No I'm not afraid of you

MARVIN: I should hope not. I've just lost my father. You'd have to be mad to be afraid of me

MR SMITH: Yes but I'm not

MARVIN: What then? The future? Are you afraid of what the future may bring

MR SMITH: Not particularly

MARVIN: The past then?

MR SMITH: No

MARVIN: No, of course not, that's all dead and gone

Pause.

Oh come on then, don't keep us all guessing for Christ's sake!

MR SMITH: Do you mind if we finish this and we can talk about it later

MARVIN: Don't be touchy with me, I'm grieving

MR SMITH: Alright I'm sorry

BUBBLES: Marvin, do you want me to put my arms around you and you rest your head on me. Come on, like when we were little

MARVIN: (*Does so.*) I'm so scared Bubbles, everything's so horrible. Daddy's dead, I've eaten Mrs Bulima and then there's that other fellow

BUBBLES: Mr Baron

MARVIN: Yes, he's dead too. And I don't know what to do or what's going to happen next. And Mr Smith treats me as if he doesn't know me, but when he first appeared on the scene I was the only one spoke up for him

BUBBLES: I have to ask you Marvin, Why did you eat –

MARVIN: She wanted me to, join in she said, don't be shy, I like to share –

BUBBLES: What?

MARVIN: She was eating herself you see

BUBBLES: Was she?

MARVIN: I thought it was strange but it would have been rude to refuse. "I honestly find everything so delicious" she said, I can hear her now. She was a nice woman

BUBBLES: Yes she was

MARVIN: She just wanted to do her own thing. And some people of course don't like that

BUBBLES: No, they don't

MARVIN: Hers were qualities I would be proud to have myself. She had soul

I remember her last words, they were; "people should be nice to each other" and I.. found myself agreeing

MR SMITH: I agree with that. I know you think I don't but I do

MARVIN: I just suppose though, that she wasn't very...

BUBBLES: Clever

MARVIN: No, she wasn't very clever. She died in a ridiculous manner with those anodyne words on her lips

MR SMITH: What better way

MARVIN: What?

MR SMITH: Nothing

BUBBLES walks away.

MR SMITH: Where's Bubbles gone?

MARVIN: She's walked away

MR SMITH: Don't you think your calamitous behaviour has upset her Marvin?

MARVIN: Don't you think your miserable face has offended everyone you've ever met? Don't you think your, you know, the way you shuffle about moaning all the time is an offence to the sky you turn your back on? You're inviting rain. You are a rain dance. Don't you want to help me protest against injustice? Don't you care anymore? She can see you are no longer a man. Your hand is in the cash register. You live in the wrong part of town, in the wrong town, in the wrong country. You're the wrong colour, the wrong age, you don't like anyone but you think you are doing society a favour, but just at what point will you bear witness? You'd like to be canonised first, isn't that right?

MR SMITH: Ok, call her back. I shall take your advice. What was your advice?

MARVIN: I don't remember giving you any advice

MR SMITH: Alright. I shall hence forth listen to the voice inside me which says; why make things difficult for yourself, do a little bit of what you want

MARVIN: You have a voice that says that?

MR SMITH: I do. We'll see how it goes. Firstly I shall call back Bubbles. Bubbles! Please come back!

BUBBLES: (*Comes back.*) Well?

MR SMITH: Let me be your dog. The shadow of your dog

BUBBLES: So, you're in this mood. I'll come back when you're yourself again

BUBBLES walks away.

MARVIN: That didn't get you very far did it

MR SMITH: She'll be back. Secondly I shall exhume my
three friends and bring them back to life

MARVIN: I don't find you very sincere in this mood.
They're not your friends, except Mr Baron and he's
mad. The others you don't even like

MR SMITH: Exhume boy, exhume! Don't quibble! Great
things are afoot!

MARVIN: Shall I dig them out?

MR SMITH: That's it, take the shovel and dig. A bit of
honest sweat won't harm you

MARVIN: But what then? What will you do then?

MR SMITH: When Bubbles comes I shall marry her.
We will ride away and live in a big house

MARVIN: You already live with her in a big house

MR SMITH: A bigger house. With all my favourite
things

MARVIN: And then?

MR SMITH: I'll give money to everyone

MARVIN: Money can't bring happiness

MR SMITH: I will bring money and justice to everyone
I will be judge and jury

MARVIN: Then what?

MR SMITH: And I shall help everyone to find their
favourite religion and build beautiful temples
everywhere

MARVIN: People like sport

MR SMITH: I will build sports temples

MARVIN: People like mountain climbing, people like
   rifle ranges, wrestling, pig fighting, murder rape pillage

MR SMITH: Dig man, dig! I shall as judge condemn the
   wicked and then persuade them to the ways of goodness

MARVIN: I see, This is quite typical of a depressive like
   you, to harbour a secret desire to play God

MR SMITH: God? If He existed he would be one of the
   first I would have to punish for his crimes. If there is
   any moral law He has broken it, if anyone has

MARVIN: But He made us Mr Smith

MR SMITH: That is the least of his crimes, his greatest
   of course was to make Himself, author of all ills

MARVIN: But Mr Smith, God gave us Freedom

MR SMITH: Freedom to do what?

MARVIN: To choose good of course

MR SMITH: But strangely our natures prevent us
   from doing so. So what kind of freedom is it you are
   prevented from ever enjoying? That of the prisoner
   looking through the bars

MARVIN: But learning to love God is the key to those bars

MR SMITH: Yes, if we take His word for it that He is
   good, against all the evidence if I may say so

MARVIN: You say God isn't good?

MR SMITH: Aren't we to seek his face in his creation?

MARVIN: Has existence made you indignant Mr Smith?
   What a monster of pride you are

MR SMITH: God made me did He?

MARVIN: Yes

MR SMITH: The good part or the bad part?

MARVIN: The good part. The bad in you is your sinfulness

MR SMITH: Then why is it that in order not to be indignant at God's cruelty I have to ignore my good part, which is the only part He accepts responsibility for?

MARVIN: It's all a bit peevish Mr Smith, crude and narrow minded. Not what I'd expect from a man of your sophistication

MR SMITH: Dig boy, dig!

MARVIN: I'm not digging up Mrs Bulima, she's just a skeleton

MR SMITH: Dig! Dig!

MARVIN: I don't think Bubbles is going to like this Mr Smith (*Pause.*)

MR SMITH: You're right. Bury them again

MARVIN: Too late!

He lifts the lids of the three disinterred coffins.

Pause.

MR SMITH: Well?

MARVIN: They're dead

MR SMITH: Oh

MARVIN: What did you expect?

MR SMITH: Drag them out, let's have a look

MARVIN does so.

Get up you mad birds! You white stones! Get up, speak!

MR GREENHOUSE: – And so it came to pass that the man who had driven the sun into the ground and eaten his father's lover was in turn himself driven into the ground by the spirit of his dead father who said (*To MARVIN.*); My son, your light is darkness, your future past, your hope in vain, your vanity destruction, your life is apedom aped of an ape, your mockery is mocked, your mocked mockery is soon forgotten. Drugery's warm hand is already upon you. Meanwhile the loser, Mr Smith, he became the judge and jury of all the world.

MR SMITH: I am judge and jury of all the world

MR GREENHOUSE: – and he sang to us making us all free, but freedom soon turned to slavery and he said "let me be judge no more" but no voice heard him for all the voices were quiet and spoke no more

And the guard at the door, he dropped dead and was never seen again

Or, his old friend says he went with him with his funny voice, running in the countryside to help him find rabbits

Out in a damp field.

MR SMITH: Here rabbits! Here rabbits! (*Pause.*) There are no rabbits

Back in the summer meadow.

MR SMITH: So what do we do now Mr Greenhouse, revived as you are from the grave

MR GREENHOUSE: Start all over again I expect

MR SMITH: Well. I would be exaggerating if I said I couldn't bear it

MR GREENHOUSE: No, it's not too bad is it, we're lucky

MR SMITH: Who is?

MR GREENHOUSE: You, me, our friends, people like us, our class, this country, Europe, the West, the World, the Solar System, the Universe

MR SMITH: I'm not sure at what point but I feel you have started to exaggerate

MR GREENHOUSE: I know it. It's such a conundrum

BUBBLES returns.

MR SMITH: Ah Bubbles. Well, how am I doing?

BUBBLES: Not bad I suppose

Pause.

MR SMITH: What about you?

BUBBLES: Yes?

MR SMITH: What will you do when you are my age? How will you deal with it?

BUBBLES: Oh I don't expect to get that old

MR SMITH: Ah.

*   *   *

Beside a broad flowing river, in a city.

MR BARON: Mr Smith

MR SMITH: Mr Baron

MR BARON: See how the river runs Mr Smith, so lovely

MR SMITH: (*Pause.*) Yes

MR BARON: On your way to work Mr Smith? Are those the design plans in your briefcase?

MR SMITH: No, my briefcase is empty now Mr Baron, no more designs

MR BARON: This is where that poor boy was killed, murdered for his religion, his race, swept away by the river. I didn't know the boy of course. He was a stranger, alien in his ways, ignorant of the do's and the don't's, perhaps not even willing to learn, who knows?

MR SMITH: Yes

MR BARON: But that's no reason to kill him. No reason to throw him into the river to drown

MR SMITH: You're absolutely right Mr Baron

MR BARON: I am right. I've been thinking about it

MR SMITH: What have you thought?

MR BARON: I've been thinking in terms of Freedom

MR SMITH: Freedom Mr Baron? Hard to define

MR BARON: Indeed. But do we need more definitions Mr Smith? There are already so many

MR SMITH: What can we have instead?

MR BARON: Lists. We could have lists instead

MR SMITH: What kind of list would that be?

MR BARON: A list of all the different things

MR SMITH: We should need a very long list indeed

MR BARON: Yes but what I say is, what is wrong with a long list? Let it be long in the name of Christ, let it be long enough to include all that is there, before it all disappears. And if you don't want to name something then don't, leave it out, but don't say it doesn't exist. If I jump into this river now and say that I am a fish, then let me swim like a fish, feed me with fish food, sing fish songs to me and catch me on your hooks, but don't say "fish have gills Mr Baron, not lungs"; Fry me if you like, pour remoulade on my back, but don't say I didn't love water! Because I DIED when you took me out of the water so I do love water!

MR SMITH: But, well... Mr Baron, you would sink

MR BARON: Yes, I am fat and I would sink. But did anyone consider that I might want to sink. I might want to end my days with that boy for example, to share his fate. My actions are my own, they are not to be guessed at. Do you like what I am saying?

MR SMITH: Yes I like it. But you seem sad Mr Baron

MR BARON: Yes, I am a little sad, and frankly my boy, I don't know what to say

MR SMITH: I don't know what to say either

The End.

A LITTLE SATIRE

A LITTLE SATIRE was first performed at the Gate Theatre on the 10th May 1997. It was directed by David Farr, with the following cast:

Paul Ebsworth

Simon Finch

Anne Firbank

Mark Gilles

Ramm Gray

Eliza Hunt

Rose Keegan

Peter Sproole

Alastair Treville

Penny Dimond

Josh Darcy

Characters

JOHN

NORMAL

RIGHT

HONOURABLE

MEMBER

BOY

SADIE

NARRATOR

VOX

POP

MR. FYFFY

BESSIE

CILLA

KENNY

GORDON

ALGY

MY LORD BISHOP

DIMBLEBY

DISCHARGE

NOSE

REDDITCH

VOICE

2ND MAN

JOHN: Normal... I think it's time for another election

NORMAL: But you had one an hour ago John

JOHN: Election, I said

*   *   *

RIGHT: Quick boys! let's run, The angry populace is bound to want justice

HONOURABLE: You know how they love justice!

MEMBER: They'll want answers!

RIGHT: You know how they love answers

HONOURABLE: Let's run to where there is no justice and no answers!

MEMBER: Quick, to the housing estates! We want doorsteps!

RIGHT: Look! A sad crowd of crying people!

HONOURABLE: What's wrong you small bods?

SADIE: They've prorogued our parliament. Now we have no-one and nothing and no-one loves us and looks after us, to speak up for us and our rights and to get us justice and fair and square and everything what is ours and belonging to us

RIGHT: You mad crew! Where is your articulate spokesperson, quick before we beat you

BOY: Me, it's me. The weeks drag on, the wind blows silent

HONOURABLE: That's enough! I have a plan. You must vote for us and we will bring back all those good things. Meanwhile boys, chew on these (*Bananas*.)

*   *   *

Enter three men trying to peel a banana.

NARRATOR: What are you going to do when you've peeled that banana boys?

VOX: We're going to give it to our friends of course mister

POP: Here is our friends

BOY: (*Comes wobbling from the sight of the banana they have thrown on the floor.*) Hang on! I go all wibbley when I see that. Hold me!

VOX: We'll hold you mister

*   *   *

Enter three men trying to put a banana back in its skin.

RIGHT: What are you going to do when you've succeeded putting that banana back in its skin boys?

VOX: We're going to stick it up our bum, mister

RIGHT: But boys boys, it's going to be all squashy with the way you're putting your fingers in it

POP: Not half as squashy as it's going to be when we've stuck it up our nasty bum, Mister

RIGHT: Alright. Now I'd like you to take this penny and put it safely in your bank

VOX: Alright we will

They try to put it up their bum.

RIGHT: No, no, not like that, that's your bum! Don't you have anywhere you can invest it. Or you could buy a video or a car. You know what a car is don't you boys?

POP: Yes, we love cars

RIGHT: You know what love is don't you boys?

VOX: Yes, we love our country

RIGHT: You know what your country is don't you boys?

VOX: Yes it's where we go shopping for plastic curtain rails on Saturday afternoon in the car

RIGHT: You are beginning to understand. Now if you love your country you are going to need somewhere to park, am I right?

POP: Yes Mister

RIGHT: Now that is what my friends and I can provide

VOX: You mean you know a space?

RIGHT: I wouldn't go so far as to say that, but if you purchase this bag of cement from me I will provide you with a voucher to build one wherever you like

*   *   *

NARRATOR: Mrs Poor, Mr Empty, and little-boy-broken-home, all met at the hustings one day where a very nice man called George was explaining parity with the yen, when Mrs Poor asked George if he thought it was possible to live on two shillings and sixpence per week. George, quite rightly, said that this was not the point

RIGHT: I expect you want double that!

SADIE: Yes, and triple and quadruple!

RIGHT: Listen Mrs Pig –

SADIE: Mrs Poor

RIGHT: You've got all your white durables haven't you Mrs Floor?

SADIE: Mrs Flower. Yes I have

RIGHT: And each day you waste your money on your plastic comestibles Mrs Lower?

SADIE: Mrs Slower. I do. Pizza is my favourite

RIGHT: And you've got your black unbearables
  Mrs Slaughter?

SADIE: Mrs Laughter. One in every room, the kiddies stare
  at it all day bless 'em

RIGHT: Then more money would mean more of the same,
  Mrs Grafter

SADIE: Mr Shafter! How dare you say I'm not worth it
  after all I've done for this country

RIGHT: Let me explain. What would you do with your life
  if you had the chance?

SADIE: I'd send my kids to school to learn and get a trade
  I'd get a job myself and earn my keep and when I'm old
  I'll buy presents for my grandchildren

RIGHT: Call that a life? That's just existing. Don't you
  have any imagination Mrs Poor?

SADIE: No, none at all

*   *   *

MEMBER: Hello little boy, what's wrong?

BOY: I've killed my mummy

MEMBER: Oh dear. Then I'd like you to volunteer to go to
  prison forever

BOY: Alright

MEMBER: And you have to wear this around your neck and
  sign this piece of paper. It's a pretty photograph of you

BOY: Ok

MEMBER: We'll all sleep safely in our beds now won't we
  Ma?

  Now don't be nervous little boy, I'd like to ask you a few
  questions for this study I'm doing

BOY: Ok Mister

MEMBER: First... who is the Prime Minister of this your
   lovely country?

BOY: Benny the squirrel

MEMBER: Correct. I can see we're going to get along
   splendidly Now, what is your favourite book in the
   electronic library in your school?

BOY: The electronic coca-cola book

MEMBER: What happens when you mix sodium
   metabisulphate with glucose?

BOY: I get the shits

MEMBER: Good. Geography now, Where is Spain?

BOY: It's on holiday with my dad

MEMBER: And lastly, do you know anywhere quiet where
   we can go for a little drink together?

*   *   *

A windy heath on the campaign trail a huge banana enters, MR FYFFY.

MR FYFFY: Where is everyone? It seems so empty.
   Where's all the May day colour, Not a mouse stirring.
   Where are all my friends and mateys? Is this Knutsford
   Heath? Is this the bottom to which there is no top?

VOX: It's Mr Fyffy

POP: Thou art a scholar, you speak to it

VOX: So, you had your hand in the till

POP: Too right! His virtues in the general censure take
   corruption from that particular fault

MR FYFFY: O that this too sullied flesh would melt!

VOX: It is offended. See, it stalks away!

POP: (*Smelling MR FYFFY.*) There is something rotten Mr Fyffy

MR FYFFY: If you think I smell it only bodes a strange corruption to our state, I am but a prologue to the omen coming on

VOX: Speak if thou art privy to the country's fate that foreknowing mightst avoid

POP: He beckons, maybe he wants to whisper

VOX: He says successive ministers of state have gone hot and full to the skirts of Belgium and various other places and here and there sharked up a list of lawless resolutes and the heavy headed revel makes us taxed and traduced of other nations and it's not remotely democratic

POP: Heavens! What shall we do?

VOX: (*Listens to the whisper.*) He says we should recover with a strong hand from the Friesian and the Frank those lands lost by terms compulsory

POP: What happens if we don't?

VOX: (*Listens.*) He says they might deprive us of our sovereignty with Reasons and draw us into madness with wicked wit and gifts that have the power to seduce

POP: Well, he's a fine one to talk. Ask him if he knows there's soon to be a rummage in the land

VOX: Do you know there's soon to be a rummage in the land?

POP: He started like a guilty thing upon a fearful summons

MR FYFFY: O I must render myself up!

POP: Alas, poor banana!

VOX: I'll see thee at Knutsford then?

MR FYFFY: At Knutsford

There's just one more thing

VOX: Yes?

MR FYFFY: There's never a villain at Knutsford but he's an arrant knave

POP: There needs no banana come from the grave to tell us this.

*   *   *

NARRATOR: And now, back to the marginals.

MEMBER: Hello little boy, what's wrong?

BOY: My prosthetic head has burst and there was blood all over the whole road

MEMBER: Very nasty indeed, But you're a strange fella and no mistake. Does your mummy know you're out?

BOY: She sent me out to buy a bag of chicken wings from the plate o mex but two big girls came and stole me and put me in a slot machine to buy those rubber underwears, that's when my head burst

MEMBER: What you need lad is education

BOY: Roasted please mister

MEMBER: Your sad tale has exhausted me. Do you know of a mattress we could lie down on?

BOY: My mum peed on mine, but we could sleep on the video machine

MEMBER: Do you often sleep on the video machine, you poor deprived little ragamuffin?

BOY: Well,

MEMBER: Enough! Take me there sad wretch from a broken home, take me at once to your housing estate, You see small boy, I am on the run

BOY: My big sister Ruby has an ocean of fat under her skirt she told me. You can sleep there if you don't mind the smell of fish...

MEMBER: Foolish boy, there are no fish in the ocean, only tiddlers. What a wicked world

*   *   *

BESSIE: Hey mister, what are you doing under my skirt

MEMBER: I was checking your quota

BESSIE: There's nothing wrong with my quota that a bit of deep sea electromagnetic stun bleeper trawling wouldn't sort out

MEMBER: Mmm, a lively lass. Perhaps I could take this opportunity of canvassing your vote – I stand on a platform of standards – Do you know this one? – (*Sings.*) "To dream, the impossible dream"

BESSIE: Wind your neck in mate, you're interfering with my heavy flow. It's my life, you know

MEMBER: You sexy independent girl you! And to prove my love I'm going to give you this (*A banana.*)

BESSIE: Ooerr! What is it?

MEMBER: Your happiness

BESSIE: That's what they all say. It doesn't look like much to me

MEMBER: It's not what you've got it's what you do with it

BESSIE: (*In tears.*) But why do I have to do things with it?

MEMBER: To save the world. Don't you know it's overheating?

BESSIE: No

MEMBER: Don't they brainwash you at school at all? Soon all the ice will melt and you know what that will mean?

BESSIE: No more frozen pizzas?

MEMBER: Exactly. Now if you cool this happiness fruit by putting it inside your body my interest rates will rise thus preventing the global economy from overheating

BESSIE: It's a lie. I can't get that inside me. I'm only likkel

MEMBER: Nonsense. You've swallowed bigger ones than that, I can tell

BESSIE: Only for money, there is a maximum limit to what a girl can take

MEMBER: £3.86 do?

BESSIE: I don't know

MEMBER: Think of it as an act of charity

BESSIE: Eh?

MEMBER: Like giving comic relief

BESSIE: I did a singer once

MEMBER: That's it

BESSIE: I'm a first timer, be gentle with me

MEMBER: I will be. Would you like to see my pledge?

BESSIE: Alright

MEMBER: Here (*A manifesto rolled up.*)

BESSIE: It's all red and bloated

MEMBER: Yes

BESSIE: But it's smaller than I imagined

MEMBER: Don't worry it will grow once we're in

BESSIE: We?

MEMBER: Didn't I mention my friends? how remiss of me...

* * *

CILLA: Welcome to this evening's free Blind holiday in Bonanza Country. Tonight's guests include the usual clutch of greedy little tarts with no brains selected from You The People. Come on down Bessie!

BESSIE: Hello boys, are you pleased to see me or is that just your poll showing?

CILLA: And now the Treasures she has to choose between; Careful Kenny Clerk who claims to offer you Bessie a safe pair of hands, Mad Bad Lord Gordon Gaping fish who also offers a safe pair and last but not least, a friend of Paddy Peanuts, who offers you just that. What else have you got to offer boys?

KENNY: I can promise a tight fiscal squeeze

CILLA and AUDIENCE: Whooooa!

GORDON: I can offer a tight fiscal squeeze too, plus, I can promise that I'll get her on the job and keep her there

CILLA: Whoooa! How will you pay for that Gordon?

GORDON: Well, I'm expecting that when I shake her tree there will be an abundant windfall

CILLA: Whoooa! And you little boy, what have you got to offer this lass?

HONOURABLE: I'm the quiet studious type so I'll keep her indoors training up her skills. We'll share a bag of peanuts beside the fire

CILLA: Sounds cosy doesn't it Bessie?

BESSIE: Mm yeah, a bit too cosy for me

CILLA: And how will you pay for em... the bag of peanuts?

HONOURABLE: Well, they're so cheap, I think I can raise a penny towards it

CILLA: Mm, sounds like that's all you can raise, but we'll see, you have to watch these quiet ones. And Ken, once you get Bessie into your clutches

BESSIE: – Not likely!

CILLA: Will you be the kind who, once you've conned her into a date with your soft soap you'll, like, try to have your wicked way with her?

KENNY: No I'll take her to a posh restaurant first for a few beers

CILLA: And how will you pay for it?

KENNY: Oh that will be easy, because it will be pudding time

CILLA: – Eh? You're a cunning one. He's a bit cryptic inne'?

KENNY: I mean Cilla, that once she gets her lips around my blood pudding, revenues will rise

CILLA: Whoooa! So Bessie, which one do you choose?

BESSIE: There's not much to choose between 'em really Cilla, can I have a gang bang?

CILLA: Naughty. No, you've got to choose

BESSIE: Ok then. Well I've heard the pudding time line before and, well, it normally means muggins here ends up holding the baby, so not him. Mister peanuts, he seems to have a one track mind beneath that one track exterior so I'll take Mad Bad Gordon because he's original but he'd better keep his hands to himself because, as my dad says, Never go near a shaft unless you're in a union!

CILLA: – Come out Gordon

BESSIE: Oh My God!

CILLA: So Gordon – Bessie

BESSIE: Oh Crikey! Well he looks a bit shifty, I hope I don't get taken for a ride

CILLA: What do you say to that Gordon?

GORDON: I say; Bessie, it's always a bit of a gamble, and I can't promise a steeple chase, but by the looks of her, if we get past the post I won't be the first to have removed her maiden's handicap

CILLA: Saucy

BESSIE: (*As they go off.*) I'd think I'd be better of with a bag of nuts

*   *   *

SADIE: Oh I can't make head nor tail of this, with you all squabbling amongst yourselves

MEMBER: There is a clear choice facing you Sadie on election day. You can choose ignorance, squalor, secrecy, isolation, alienation, aimlessness, emptiness, lack of vision and hypocrisy. Or you could choose not to stay at home with your family but instead to come out and vote. At least it would get you away from them for half an hour

*   *   *

RIGHT: Now little boy, you look intelligent. Tell us what we should do

HONOURABLE: Yes, what do you want, just name it, anything you like it's yours!

BOY: Beautiful architecture and culture and old things and new things and peace and freedom and homes and food and fields and flowers and we give presents to everyone and stay home Sundays and give thanks to the creator and talk to all the happy animals and trees and walk in the paths of wisdom and a quiet spirit and dream of the mists and forests that covered our land and the sunshine and old stones of other lands where our forefathers were and be happy and one with all peoples our brothers and sisters and we remember old dances and old songs can you do that for us mister?

RIGHT: Nno, but in two years we could be looking at a new Asda store built in your area

BOY: OK, that will do

RIGHT: Marvellous. And you can be the airfreshener boy in the toilets for the drive-in customers

BOY: Oooh must I then be clipped to the urinal?

RIGHT: For your own comfort in the workplace you will be secured to the toilet bowl with a one piece plastic clip which will be made in Britain at a competitive price creating 17 jobs in Newtownnewtown of which we may be proud

BOY: But the lovely pinefresh piss-cleaner liquid I will spurt from my mouth, will that be made here too?

RIGHT: No boy, that will be produced in Thailand in a high tech, low-spec, low cost, labour-free plant that leaks into a filthy Thai river and cleaning it with pine freshness

BOY: I'll run home and tell ma. She'll be so proud

RIGHT: How old are you sonny?

BOY: Thirty-six

HONOURABLE: You're a credit to your probation officer

RIGHT: Just show us what you can do and in seven years you could own your own trouser press and open a conference centre and be a multi billionaire

BOY: Yes I will, I will, I think I really will, what a beautiful vista

RIGHT: So remember we're putting the 'back' back in Britain. Tell your friends

HONOURABLE: Who can we help next? Do you know anyone, small boy, who would like to build on what has been achieved?

BOY: em...

*   *   *

A poor old pisser sits in a chair.

RIGHT: Oh dear, what's happened here?

Enter ALGY.

ALGY: Hello friends

RIGHT: Now Algy admit it, you've got a sleepy bowel

ALGY: Alright I admit it

RIGHT: Now Algy we'd like you to be our Nation's Future

ALGY: Alright I will

HONOURABLE: Good. Now, we'd like you to take this hosepipe and put it into your wife's honey pot when you get home

ALGY: Alright I will

RIGHT: And we'll pay for the ambulance

ALGY: Alright. Thank you chaps

HONOURABLE: Good. Now, you see this old pisser?

ALGY: Yes, I see him loud and clear

RIGHT: He's gone and pissed it all away so we're not going to help him, Are you pleased Algy?

ALGY: I'm very pleased, thank you chaps

HONOURABLE: Don't you go yet Algy, stay a while

ALGY: Alright I will

RIGHT: We'd like you to ask this rotten man why he's pissed it all away?

ALGY: Why did you do it!?

HONOURABLE: Go on Algy

ALGY: Why did you piss all your money away?

RIGHT: That's it Algy!

*   *   *

HONOURABLE: Hello matey

NARRATOR: What's that you're wearing?

HONOURABLE: A party dress

NARRATOR: Poor cow. And er...

HONOURABLE: Well I want everyone to have one

NARRATOR: Thank you and er...

HONOURABLE: I shall pay for it. By charging you one penny

NARRATOR: One penny only?? Amazing. That's very cheap

HONOURABLE: It's a cheap party

*   *   *

RIGHT: Let's just start another country somewhere else

MEMBER: Yes, where?

RIGHT: Next to this little boy

BOY: Oh please don't mister!

MEMBER: Don't you want to be next to a new country, boy?

BOY: No mister

RIGHT: Have you no ambition? Exercise your options lad, get up, get a lifestyle, do you realise you are blocking a potential jobs superhighway? Don't they teach you anything in school

BOY: Peanuts, Mister

MEMBER: And yet, and yet, your shoes are so promising, and that denim nappy you are wearing! What's it all for eh?

BOY: They're better innit?

RIGHT: Have you ever heard of judicial reform?

BOY: (*Laughs leerily.*)

MEMBER: Now little lad this new country we're going to start is going to be on a big ship and you have been chosen to be trainee cabin boy

BOY: How long for Mister?

RIGHT: Three years with parole

BOY: Thanks. Will I learn a trade?

MEMBER: That depends on the other inmates. But I can promise you one thing

BOY: What's that Mister?

RIGHT: Eternal unemployment

BOY: Is that the same as National Salvation?

MEMBER: Precisely lad and we're all very grateful for your little sacrifice

*   *   *

MEMBER: Why are you weeping?

HONOURABLE: I've just read this report on the terrible poverty and inequality in our society

MEMBER: That's dreadful

HONOURABLE: This little lad for example has no brain, no food, no parents, no house, no morals, no culture, he's starving before our eyes!

MEMBER: There's only one thing for it

HONOURABLE: Give him a large pocket money rise?

MEMBER: No

HONOURABLE: Build a little house for him?

MEMBER: No

HONOURABLE: Educate him???

MEMBER: No

HONOURABLE: Feed the little fella?

MEMBER: No

HONOURABLE: What then O master?

MEMBER: We are a party of practical politics. We deal in the possible

HONOURABLE: What shall we do then?

MEMBER: We shall abolish the hereditary peerage

HONOURABLE: (*Tugging his ear.*) Hear that boy? Injustice is gone forever

BOY: Thank you sir

HONOURABLE: In a few years the whole of the upper house will be political appointees. Your troubles are over

MEMBER: (*Aside.*) Of course they say you can't eat democracy but I'm going to damn well try

BOY: (*Aside.*) They're forgetting one thing... My Lord Bishops...

NARRATOR: My Lord bishop has come to ask if it might not be possible...

MY LORD BISHOP: If it might not be possible, forgive me for mentioning it, possible to do something for poor little Johnny here who God Bless him, has no school no god no future no memory, all he has is luxury trainers and a head full of shit.

HONOURABLE: He's a cheeky little chappie and I know I speak for my whole party when I wish him well and I would be the first to say that in the sight of god he is as good as me. I am a man. The soul is your department vicar, leave his body to me...

MEMBER: Bishop. May I call you Davy, or Dave, or D.? We have not forgotten this boy and by the time he's 47 he'll be paying tax and national insurance like everyone else even if I have to pay it for him out of my own expense account. That is my pledge. In the meantime would you all stand at the back of the shop so I can see my customers

MY LORD BISHOP: Would you just slip that magazine under my cassock sonny?

BOY: But that's stealing

MY LORD BISHOP: Don't worry, property is theft and theft is evil

NARRATOR: (*Points at confused BOY's head.*) Thinks; "Does this mean a pocket money rise?"

BOY: ... or should I, instead of sniffing glue, have looked deeper into Morals and Political Economy?

*   *   *

NARRATOR: The plot so far; Our three heroes have given the Horrible Family the slip

RIGHT: We have escaped anyway haven't we mateys?

HONOURABLE: Yes we have

MEMBER: Yes we have

RIGHT: Is this Mr Hogg?

HONOURABLE: Yes he's buried under the nation's greatest brains

MEMBER: Is that a stubborn grin on his face or is his smile just leaking into the water table?

RIGHT: Oh dear! Do you think it will trickle down?

HONOURABLE: Well, ... on past evidence we have very little to worry about

*   *   *

SADIE: None of them do anything for me

RIGHT: What do you want you old bitch, a holiday in Bermuda?

SADIE: I've worked all my life...

RIGHT: What about everyone else, a whole country full of people

SADIE: Sod the country I want a bigger pension

RIGHT: Could I interest you in a babanannaba? (*Hands her a banana.*)

SADIE: Oh yes! I could wash my face with it! (*Does so.*) Mm, seventeen years of married life. I look back and I can hardly believe it

RIGHT: It's been astonishing hasn't it

HONOURABLE: Excuse me sir there's a starving Hottentot at the door

RIGHT: Tell him they were delicious and I'd like two dozen more

HONOURABLE: At once O she who must be obeyed

MEMBER: So Sadie tell us what you think, tell us what you'd like

SADIE: I –

RIGHT: Let us tell you first what is our governing principle

MEMBER: You see Sadie, it's this; you have to take the place as you find it, it's not a virgin piece of land, it's not a virgin country Sadie

RIGHT: Far from it

MEMBER: Yes far from it

RIGHT: We can't just start from scratch

MEMBER: We inherit the

SADIE: the?

MEMBER: the road

RIGHT: yes the road

MEMBER: If there's 9/10 of a road Sadie what do you do eh?

SADIE: I –

RIGHT: Do you close it and waste all the loving effort

MEMBER: – and money

RIGHT: and money – your money Sadie, that has gone into making it, incomplete and imperfect as it is

MEMBER: Or do you complete it

RIGHT: Finish it off

MEMBER: Do the last tenth, turning 9/10 of a road.

RIGHT: Into a complete road from A –

MEMBER: To B Hey presto!

RIGHT: Tell us Sadie

MEMBER: Now there's just one thing that worries us Sadie – and I think there's cross party support on this one

RIGHT: We're as one on this Sadie

MEMBER: And that is, this

RIGHT: What is the meaning of life?

SADIE: Wh – ?

RIGHT: Tell us

MEMBER: Tell us

RIGHT: Tell us

MEMBER: You don't know?

RIGHT: You disappoint us

MEMBER: You're not answering our question

RIGHT: You scum Sadie

Long pause. SADIE thinks long and hard.

MEMBER: Sadie

SADIE: Yes

MEMBER: Can I interest you in a banana?

RIGHT: Now Sadie, it's your turn again

SADIE: In a green society

RIGHT: What does it mean "a green society" –

MEMBER: I don't think it means anything at all

RIGHT: Ha ha ha

MEMBER: Ha ha ha

RIGHT: Ha ha ha ha

MEMBER: Ha ha ha ha ha

RIGHT: Ha ha ha ha ha

MEMBER: Ha ha ha ha ha ha

RIGHT: Ha ha ha ha ha ha ha

SADIE: I would have two cars instead of one

They look at her in wonder.

SADIE: You see, the gap between the poor on the one hand

RIGHT: Yes

SADIE: And the rich on the other

MEMBER: Yes

SADIE: Has...

RIGHT: Has what?

SADIE: It's bigger

MEMBER: Bigger? Bigger than what?

SADIE: You're getting me confused

RIGHT: What's in a gap Sadie?

SADIE: Nothing

MEMBER: A load of fuss about nothing

RIGHT: (*In a whisper.*) The politics of envy

MEMBER: Try again Sadie

RIGHT: Yes try again

SADIE: What about the unions?

MEMBER: What about them?

SADIE: They're too strong

RIGHT: But we've abolished them Sadie

SADIE: Oh, I don't know, answer the question

MEMBER: I think what Sadie is trying to say is when is all this bickering about taxation going to stop and the whole system abolished and replaced with one which is fair and doesn't cost anything, Is that right?

SADIE: Yes, yes that's what I mean

RIGHT: I'm afraid Sadie that isn't possible

SADIE: Yes but why don't you answer the question?

RIGHT: Ok, let me answer it in my own way

SADIE: No you answer it my way

RIGHT: What is the question?

SADIE: I don't know

MEMBER: I think what Sadie is trying to say is when is all this bickering about policy going to stop so we can get down to discussing the issues

SADIE: No I'm sick of the issues, I want policies

MEMBER: You want policies?

SADIE: Yes why isn't anyone interested in what ordinary people's policies are

RIGHT: They haven't got any have they?

DIMBLEBY: I don't know, have the people got any policies

SADIE: Why doesn't anyone answer my question?

DIMBLEBY: Someone else in the audience?

NOSE: Yes

DIMBLEBY: Yes, the man with the enormous nose with the snot coming out of it

NOSE: Oh I'm sorry. Does the panel realise that as we speak an area the size of Wales is being used for sheep farming, small to medium sized industry and caravan sites? And do they not agree that the only way out of the mess we are in is to have a full and ambitious programme to keep the base rate of income tax around twenty percent, to cut unemployment by 6% and improve education by involving football clubs. Surely this is the only way forward

DIMBLEBY: Anyone else? You sir yes, next to the fat person

2ND MAN: Isn't it rather hypocritical of the panel to sit there and tell us there's no such thing as government when in fact they are the government and have been the government for nearly fifty years. Isn't it time they stopped hectoring us to vote for them when in fact it's they should be voting for us

RIGHT: May I just say –

2ND MAN: – and I've also got two daughters in the state education system and if you cut their class sizes every year I've worked it out that by the year 2003 half their friends would get no education at all

DIMBLEBY: A good point but I think we're drifting off the subject a bit. The lady in the ridiculous dress, the one wearing no knickers, you madam that's right

DISCHARGE: Yes I've got a very distressing vaginal discharge which has actually broken up my family. Does the panel agree that more money should be put into development and research so that this doesn't happen

DIMBLEBY: Bobby Sox, could you answer this one

MEMBER: Yes I understand your problem and I think it shows the government are divided on defence, divided on Europe and divided on every major issue. How can we go on trusting a government to stand on its own two feet when it cannot even keep then together. And let me say this to you that if you vote for us then not only your vagina but all your gender specific parts will be in safe hands

RIGHT: May I just answer that? I'm sorry you've had this problem but what people have got to realise is that to alleviate this problem I, as an individual member have rolled back government as far as it will go and when push comes to shove in these matters the feelgood factor comes into play. May I also say that you are lucky to have a vagina at all, if this lot form the next government they'll all be closed within weeks, I read it in their manifesto

MEMBER: No you didn't

DIMBLEBY: Anyone else? You down the front with the biscuit coloured teeth

REDDITCH: Yes, can the politicians promise that I can pay no tax at all, be exempt from the law and have sex with as many women as I want including their own wives and daughters? I'm a small business man

MEMBER: Where are you from sir?

REDDITCH: Redditch

MEMBER: Yes anyone in your situation can indeed expect all that and more, certainly before the election, and in fact you can screw me as well if you like. After the election though any new government will have to look at it again and would in fact be hoping to screw you pretty hard if only out of revenge for having grovelled to you so much during the election campaign. Does that answer your question?

REDDITCH: Yes, thank you

*   *   *

A banana. Heartbeat and solemn female voice.

VOICE: This is a banana

After three days it is already yellow. After two weeks you can already peel it and reveal the soft fruit on the inside

After three weeks, it is a complete banana. 80% of all bananas are bought and sold at this stage. It can think for itself and make policy decisions. It can even have hiccoughs

After four weeks it can reverse policy decisions or remain completely silent. The slippery nature of the skin is now a fully developed feature

After five weeks it can speak up again but in a slightly different tone. It has feelings at this age

After six weeks most bananas have been either swallowed whole by gorillas or eaten in smaller bites by the people. Under present law this is legal

By seven weeks they have been regurgitated and put back in their skins, and can even be back on the trees again

We wanted to show you this process but they wouldn't let us. It was thought to be upsetting to public morals and decency

If we can't see it, should we be allowing it?

*   *   *

RIGHT: Well what are we going to do. It's not going very well

HONOURABLE: We'll play the fear card

RIGHT: Great. It worked last time

HONOURABLE: Let's try it on Algy

RIGHT: Algy

ALGY: Yes

RIGHT: Come here

ALGY: Alright I will

HONOURABLE: What would you say Algy if we were to tell you that the other lot are planning to strengthen the hand of the parish councils

ALGY: I'd shit myself. My wife is already busy most evenings. I'd never get any home comforts if you know what I mean

RIGHT: Excellent. Thank you Algy. Oh and Algernon

ALGY: Yes

RIGHT: Something for the weekend (*Gives him a banana.*)

ALGY: Alright I will

*   *   *

RIGHT: Well what are we going to do? It looks like we
    might actually lose

HONOURABLE: We'll play the fear card again

RIGHT: Algy

ALGY: Yes

RIGHT: Come here

ALGY: Alright I will

RIGHT: Nice weekend?

ALGY: (*Blushes.*)

HONOURABLE: Now what would you do if we were to tell
    you that the other lot are exactly like us?

ALGY: I'd shit myself. The past 17 years have been dreadful
    Oops, sorry

RIGHT: Never mind Algy. I think we've cracked it

*   *   *

RIGHT: Well what are we going to do? The fear factor
    hasn't worked. It seems they must have really rather
    enjoyed the past 17 years

HONOURABLE: This is becoming a little complicated

RIGHT: That's it!

HONOURABLE: What?

RIGHT: We'll confuse them

HONOURABLE: Algy

ALGY: Yes?

HONOURABLE: Come here

ALGY: Alright I will

RIGHT: What would you do if I told you that we were going to apply the principle of "if it's not hurting it's not working"

ALGY: I'd say jolly good thing, that's what I said to Mrs Algy at the weekend. I'd say You've got to be firm Painful decisions have got to be made sometimes in the interest of of of of the interests. Britain needs good strong leadership from those who have been trained to provide it. It's a matter of breeding really, as Metternich used to say...

RIGHT: That'll do Algy

HONOURABLE: So you'll be glad to hear then that in accordance with these principles we've made the very tough decision to raise the base rate of income tax to 50%. How about that?

RIGHT: What's the matter Algy?

ALGY: Is there a lavatory?

HONOURABLE: Over there

RIGHT: Do you think we've overdone it

HONOURABLE: He'll get used to it. They always do

*　　*　　*

RIGHT: Well, everything has gone very quiet. We don't see much of Algy and his wife. Not like in the old days. Actually it's a bit of a relief. What an embarrassment they were

HONOURABLE: It's one of the consolations

RIGHT: I wonder what became of him though

Enter ALGY walking past with a megaphone.

ALGY: Vote labour! Reject Tory Cruelty! Vote Labour!

*   *   *

NARRATOR: It's time to show us your versatility boys.
We've had enough of the same old thing over and over.
We don't want the citizens to be bored and feel all
hopeless and helpless. Each of you must tell a story

MEMBER: Once there was a big banana with no friends.
It was old and brown and had been shoved and squashed
in so many places it had gone soft. What a loser they
said. But no it was a winner and everyone loved it and
lived happily ever after

RIGHT: Once there was a banana with lots of friends.
It could roll around and jump up and down. Yippee,
it said, Yippee. And all the ants and flies and bugs in
its vicinity were squashed and squashed again. Then
it slipped on its skin and again and again, and nobody
liked it anymore. Goodbye they said, goodbye

HONOURABLE: Once there was a banana but nobody ate
it. Try me with peanuts, it said, boldly, but few did
because they forgot to

VOX: (*As a gorilla.*) Once there was a man who ate bananas.
He was a gorilla. He ate one, then he ate another. It kept
his stomach full, but often they hurt his tummy too. He
either burped or farted, burped or farted. Once a banana
caused him to fart out of his mouth. What a surprise he
said, You never can tell

MEMBER: Once there was a banana and it said to the
gorilla Eat me, eat me, I'll make your tummy lovely and
you won't burp or fart, at least not so much as before but
let's face it anyway that's what gorillas do so you might
do sometimes

RIGHT: Excuse me. Once there was a banana and it said, Remember me? I'm your old mate. I've been up and down your gullet so many times it's like as if we're old friends and mateys and don't you dare eat that other banana because it will rot your teeth

VOX: Once there was a gorilla and it said, But you gave me the shits so bad I thought my arse was gone forever

RIGHT: No, no said the banana, once upon a time, You needed a bloody good clean out, you'd been sitting in your tree too long, it gives you piles and I cleaned it all out, now you are slim and quick and all the envy of all the other creatures in the zoo but you're too dumb to know it, don't blow it!

VOX: But my arse is gone, said the gorilla

RIGHT: You don't need it, you can eat me and it's not like eating at all, it's like thin air. Don't you know all the parrots too, they want to eat the air like you because they want to fly like you in the branches

VOX: (*Flattered.*) Do I fly, really?

RIGHT: Of course you do, don't you feel the wind in your feathers?

VOX: Em...

NARRATOR: ... said the gorilla

RIGHT: And if you eat me now again, your old favourite, I'll show you how to shit into the feathers of the cocky parrot, from high above

VOX: I'm not sure. You're such a nasty banana rotting my guts all the time, I think I might...

RIGHT: Let me explain. What would happen if a gorilla suddenly fell from its great soaring height whilst flying because it ate the wrong food?

VOX: It would fall down and die. Oh dear oh dear, I want my arse back, what shall I do?

RIGHT: There's no helping some people, said the banana

MEMBER: Once there was a banana and it said, Don't listen to Him, he's lying

VOX: Are you telling me I can't fly you stupid little banana?

MEMBER: No, no you can fly but... what it is you see, you can fly but...

VOX: And I'm beautiful when I fly aren't I?

MEMBER: Yes, you are very beautiful when you fly but sometimes gorillas have to be careful

VOX: Oh yeah? Why?

MEMBER: Because em...

VOX: Go on, why?

MEMBER: Because... how can I put this?

VOX: Answer the question, go on

MEMBER: ... em

VOX: Because...?

MEMBER: Because their feathers get covered in shit, that's why, you stupid gorilla!

VOX: (*Tearful.*) Is that what you are saying to me?

MEMBER: Yes, yes

VOX: So I can fly...

MEMBER: Yes, yes, you can fly

VOX: ... but it's just that my feathers sometimes...

MEMBER: That's it, your feathers, your lovely feathers

VOX: My lovely feathers, my birdie feathers like the parrot's only better

MEMBER: Yes

VOX: My lovely feathers...

MEMBER: Covered in it. Now eat me for God's sake before it's too late

The gorilla does so.

MEMBER: That's it, nice gorilla. You see, you do know what's good for you

VOX: Hmm, yes. Yum. That's a lot better

*   *   *

NARRATOR: And now, a Gorilla in a different situation, some weeks later

A small gorilla, in fact a cuddly chimp, is sitting on the knee of a giant banana.

VOX: Somehow my great new banana, the new flying in the air factor like a parrot hasn't quite trickled down to me yet

MEMBER: Shut up and eat shit you little berk

The End.

A MONOLOGUE

Character

A MAN

A MONOLOGUE was first peformed at the Musée
Dauphinois, Grenoble, on 30th September 1998 with the
following cast:

A MAN, Patrick Zimmerman

A plain wooden table and a plain wooden chair. A MAN enters stage right, carrying a tray with his breakfast on it. He is dressed in dark trousers and an off-white shirt buttoned to the neck, a dark waist coat and dark jacket, plain black shoes with laces. He is dusty but formal.

He sits on the chair which is on the far side of the table facing the audience.

He looks at his breakfast, stands and walks off left.

He returns with a cup of tea with milk in it, which is on a saucer, no spoon... He sits at the table as before.

He begins eating quite slowly with a knife and fork which he takes from his inside pocket.

He stops eating, looks ahead, head slightly angled upwards, say 45°.

MAN: Hmm, dawn.

Looks at his wristwatch.

It's early

Continues eating.

Faces forwards. He is intently chewing a piece of bacon. He stops, cocks his ear, smiles gently.

The dawn chorus. Amazing variety.... (*Resumes eating.*) ... for just the one bird

Pause. He chews, swallows.

How does he do it?

Smiles, enjoying the sound.

Incredible! What a repertoire!

Eats.

Pause.

Loud noise, someone dropping a plank of wood.

He looks offstage left. Continues eating.

Second loud noise, the same.

He looks off, stage left, slightly irritated.

Continues eating.

Third loud noise, the same.

He puts down his knife and fork, stands and walks calmly off, stage left.

The sound of unintelligible mumbled conversation offstage left.

He returns, resumes eating. Stops eating... Calls off, stage left.

You'll frighten the bloody bird away with that racket!

Resumes eating.

What do they care?

Continues eating.

They dragged me here against my will. They think I'm fooled by this free breakfast and the promise of a cigarette but I'm not.

I know what's in store

It's a big day, you can do anything you like. It's a little tradition.

That's the first I've heard of it.

Then I became really excited. I saw myself sitting at the gates of Heaven with my friends or rather associates and, well – in my mind's eye it was ecstasy. I imagined us singing songs and writing poems, swapping little stories to pass the time, exchanging thoughts on this and that, you know.

(*Shouts.*) Oh please no! The dessert! The dessert!

I recoiled in horror. Who was this shouting such a thing?

First I decided to use the time to make my final protest.

Then I decided not to bother.

Then I thought I should write a few postcards to my friends and loved ones, but no. –

Then I realised that the best time is spent doing nothing very much. It's what we're all familiar with. – Some I know pretend to be busy, but I know they're only joking.. And there comes a time, when the more you do, the less you do.

In fact I am reminded of a man who appeared at the corner of my street shouting – "Stop, everyone! Please stop! The less of this, the better!" It was remarkable. People did actually stop; for a couple of seconds to look at him, then they continued about their business. Unfortunately some witty young fellow yelled back to him – "You stop!" And he did. Completely. It was as if he was turned to stone. The council had to come and remove him. He was put on the back of a lorry like a statue of a deposed tyrant. The street certainly breathed easier once he was gone. Well, the very idea!

But I shan't be like him, not at all. No, in fact I have prepared something. It was actually intended as a song but who can create a rhythm when they are scared out of their wits. My hands, as you can see, are still shaking. Well, you can imagine with the eyes of the whole world upon you, at such a time. Such an *important* time.

"Such a fantastically exciting time!" – someone in fact said to me. But I ignored the remark because this person was insane

So this is called 'A song to the Gate of Heaven'.
I originally imagined we'd all sing it together but no-one
else has turned up, not surprisingly. So try to use your
imaginations for Christ's sake or this is going to be
awful.

"To him in Hell, may my heart be to me in the house
of my heart and remain in me, – I shall refuse the cakes
of the world from east and west and from the Lake of
flowers – and in my boat for sailing up, and sailing
down, with Thee, always with Thee. – My mouth,
I shall speak with it; my two legs, I shall walk with them
– open the door to me! With your two jaws prised open
and your two blind eyes and with my feet tied together
and my legs walking by themselves – My heart gaining
power over my heart, my hands over my hands, and my
two legs walking by themselves, – whatever pleases you,
for I am imprisoned beside your gates, my heart coming
into existence – You are only my double making strong
my limbs. Don't make my name stink nor take away my
soul, for I have come from beneath the floods, the first
flood and the second flood, and the floods have been
open to me and I have rubbed shoulders with the great
ones as they danced away over the horizon and I have
waved aloft the thigh, and run up and down the banks
of the dirty canal in everlastingness. Don't let me be
consumed like the one destroyed in his moment of
strength. Let all things inert come into existence – I shall
not be carried to perform festivals of fiends or fools."

Well? Don't pretend not to be surprised. I was surprised
myself.

Be brave, wear a cheerful face, this was the advice. But
I am invaded by a sense of loss. While my remaining
time, short though it be, stretches ahead like an empty
plain. The rope, which we all face at the end, beckons
like sleep, I rejoice, I yearn for it.

It's not that I don't love the things of this earth, but all pleasures are so depleted. I long to join the ranks of the dead in their dead time to review all past moments that ever were, at my leisure

Of course there are far more dead people than there are living.

Pause.

Although on the other hand, they say the gap is narrowing. Soon there will be more living people than dead ones.

What a sad day that will be.

They're going to say of course that I have missed the point. (*Pause.*) But that is to presume there was a point to miss in the first place.

Pause.

Which there wasn't.

Pause.

A load of malarky

Pause.

Codswallop

Pause.

If there was a point it is one I am glad to have missed, lets put it that way.

He looks down at his plate and is surprised to see that he has nearly finished.

Oh, I've nearly finished!

That went down pretty quick

No trouble swallowing.

Pause.

Never did have any trouble swallowing

Pause.

I swallowed just about everything. My mother said:
"Don't swallow everything." and I promised that
I wouldn't. But I did. In fact I swallowed more than
anyone else. Amongst my generation there was no more
willing a participant than myself. As a child I remember
thinking: "They're going to really like me!"

Pause.

But no, I was wrong.

Pause.

No sooner had I grown up than society had rebelled
against itself.

Pause.

And they were all so cheap. Everything they did was
cheap. And so it goes on. Look about you, I say, look
about you.

Pause.

And they have the cheek to call me a rebel.

Pause.

Rebel my arse!

Walks off, stage right.

*Returns with a newspaper. He leans back slightly in his chair
which he pushes back from the table. He crosses his legs. He leafs
through the paper at a moderate pace, then he speeds up somewhat,
leafs backwards and forwards, then screws it up loosely and throws
it on the floor.*

What nonsense!

Pause.

Urgh

In the end I withdrew in disgust.

No.

In defeat.

... to a large house full of candles, a small personal achievement.

Pause. He looks at his plate.

Meanwhile in Africa, Starvation.

Meanwhile in London, a whole generation unable to read even their horoscopes. "What does insignificant mean?" she asked. That was the last straw. Insignificant. Legions of ghosts turning in their graves, saints and sinners alike. How I pity them!

He notices a chill, stands and goes off, stage right.

He returns wearing a green cotton jacket. He wraps it closer for warmth.

"When a man is dead," I asked my friend, "how is it that he is in no way still alive but has passed out of this world altogether, notwithstanding that he has been so much in this world before?"

"It is on account of his extinction", he replied.

"How is it" I asked again "that his projects and hopes die along with him, so that he can no longer do any action at all to complete them, but instead they will fade away and be overtaken by time?"

"It is that same extinction that will have its way" he replied.

"How is it," I asked again, "that mortification and failure are then his lot while vitality and success belong only to the living?"

"That is the contrast," he replied, "between the living and the dead. Do you not see the great hopes and beliefs entertained by the living while the dead are marked out by their want of these?"

"But why," I asked, "do the living receive invitations here and there, opportunities and encouragements, however great or small their merits, while the dead are out of the running?"

"This is because they are no longer in the race"

"But why" I persevered, "is the book the dead man has left open, closed and put away, why are the contents of his freezer thrown away as if contaminated and his collection of nails and screws and pieces of wire, left to hang a while in the dust and then thrown away as if no-one could ever need them?"

"Because these are the dead man's possessions and he has passed away"

"But isn't each man" I replied "therefore lonely and foolish in his grave and mournful that the furniture of his life is only sticks and rags now that his breath and the lumbering of his limbs are no longer there to persuade the world to give them a place. Doesn't he feel ashamed like a child who is let play the fool before bed and hears the talk resume once he has left the smoky room?"

"Every dog has his day" came his riposte.

"But these living men" says I, "are so reckless, this life they live is all destruction. Why, between them they have knocked down every thing, ploughed up beauty and torn down grandeur and homeliness alike"

"Have they not" he counters "built everything too?"
But I was too clever for him:

"No, it was the dead men did that! I pity them sleeping
in their graves, allowed to rest a century or two before
the living come a-tearing at their headstones and
wrenching their poor bones back up out of the earth,
Thinking of it now makes me want to go and lay down
beside a grave and sleep with them.

"I have another point about the dead" I added.

"What is that?"

"I prefer them" I declared.

"You do? And why is that?"

"Because they are not here. They don't offend me with
their gathering success as the living do. Their lies are
long since revealed, indeed, our present gentlemen
cannot stop boasting how they scorn them, but I long
for the day when such hollow laughter is out-bellowed
by the gales of ridicule our future judges have in store
for us"

Talking of which... (*Looks at his watch.*)

*Walks off, stage right, and returns carrying a television which he sets
on the floor before his chair so that we cannot see the screen. He sits
and watches.*

Smiles indulgently.

Smiles amused.

Laughs quietly amused

Laughs quietly, indulgently.

*Smiles, raises his eyes to the ceiling briefly as if to say "how silly
nevertheless".*

Raises his eyes to the ceiling briefly again as if to say "no this is becoming too stupid".

Drops his chin and frowns as if to say "no really this is too bad".

I can't endure this nonsense!!

Pause, watches some more. Frowns, relaxes. Frowns again.

Stop it! Stop shouting at me!! Damn!

He leaps up and turns it off.

Paces up and down in annoyance and agitation.

Sits down calmly.

I wouldn't have believed it possible.
No-one would
No-one would have imagined
But there it is.

Childhood was an unfortunate invention. Now everyone wants some of it, it's spread. Now we have to walk and talk and think exactly like children.

You wouldn't have thought it possible but there it is.

The Venerable Bede wouldn't have thought it possible but there it is.

Another plank is dropped, then a hammer and a box of nails.

He looks to the left then back again.

"Anyway, don't worry," he said "nothing changes" taking what I think is called The Philosophical Attitude –

Sawing begins offstage left.

– regardless of the facts.

Looks at his watch.

Roughly twelve minutes to go

Not everyone is in agreement though. Not quite everyone.
I know several who are not in agreement – misfits, failures
and the insane – in fact my friends and family

I should pray really. Prayer is a good possible solution –
except it will never catch on. How many of the seven
billion are worthy to raise their hearts in simplicity to
their God?

It is not for me to judge however

I dreamed I spoke with God

"Is death final?" I asked him. And He replied:

"You know how when you meet someone on a train,
you know the people you meet on trains, you know
how somehow you never really imagine them having
an existence that is not on the train, even though they
normally spend the whole journey talking about that
other existence? Well, it was just the same with Me when
I made you all. I just could never imagine you having an
existence beyond the limits of death, (even though you
spend the whole journey talking about it.) so I didn't
give you one."

"Is that true?" I asked, white-faced. "You mean there
really isn't any life after death?"

"Don't be so alarmed," God said, "There wasn't Life
before birth either, but that didn't stop you from being
born" which I thought was an enigmatic thing to say.
Surely He *meant* something?

Really, now the time has come to say what I am. I have
been many things and, may I continue to be, please his
Grace. But to you my brothers and sisters.. I am the big
momento, the souvenir, the no in a world that says yes.
Is it true, you are wondering, that I know all movements
upon this earth, that I see all and hear all.

Yes. And all that's ever been, and will be. Have no fear.
No harm can come to you for we are all part of the
same...
... the same?

Sound of a plank being dropped offstage left.

... the same Thing.

Ah God be praised for that.

Does this mean no more cancer? you ask.

I wouldn't go so far as to say that, no.

Throat cancer.
Oh!
Nasty imagination.
This is no good. What a bad start!
I talk of starting but you and I know we are near the end

Looks at his watch.

"A new tomorrow, a new today."
What I normally say to them is: –
"You think you have abolished history, maybe you have,
but it will come back to abolish you all, you can rip it
out of your books, you can tear down all the buildings,
kill all the races, silence all the languages, pour concrete
onto all your cities, and square your countryside, but it
will come creeping up upon you in your empty white
bright rooms and lay its comforting black hand on your
throats...

"It's no surprise no-one lets you anywhere near the
controls. You want to drive the bus into the wall!

"You are not on a bus my friends, you are on a slab, but
they can't afford a slab anymore because it is a waste,
and when there's a cheaper way of disposal it *will* be
used, it must be used, in the interests of hygiene and

conservation. You are in the pulveriser and your minced meat is about to be fed to the sheep"

That normally does the trick.

Not that I would want to put anyone down. Far from it.

(*Calls off, stage right.*) Someone has put sugar in my bloody tea!

... But – there have been more beautiful sounds than the sounds I am hearing now, and there are more beautiful sights than the sights I am seeing now

The dust has been swept away never to return.

Hence my resentment

Looks off, stage left.

This endless celebration! It will be the death of me!